Seek the Light that Rises in the West

MIEKE MOSMULLER

SEEK THE LIGHT
THAT RISES IN THE WEST

OCCIDENT PUBLISHERS

Original title: Zoek het licht dat opgaat in het westen

Translated by: Ruth Franssen-Mosmuller

Proofreading by: Terry Boardman

Occident Publishers
Postbox 306
5110 AH Baarle Nassau
The Netherlands
Telefoon: 00-31-13-5077240 / E-mail: info@occident-publishers.com
Internet: www.occident-publishers.com

Cover design: Ad Kroese
Graphic design: Carina van den Bergh
ISBN / EAN: 978-90-75240-27-6

CONTENT

PREFACE FOR THE ENGLISH FIRST EDITION 2012

In 2009 Gabriele Savier-Dietz, who lived in England for several years, asked me during a seminar in Hamburg if it would not be possible to have my book about Rudolf Steiner 'Der lebendige Rudolf Steiner' translated into English. At that time we saw no possibility. But a deep friendship in the understanding of anthroposophy developed between Gabriele and me.

In summer 2010 she died after a sudden illness, and we decided then to fulfil her wish. But because of the fact that my first book 'Suche das Licht, das im Abendlande aufgeht' has to be available for readers of the book about Rudolf Steiner, we publish this one first. It will soon be followed by 'The living Rudolf Steiner'. I thank Ruth Franssen-Mosmuller for her translations and Terry Boardman for his careful proofreading of both translations.

In 'Seek the light...' I discribed the transsubstantiation of thinking, as it came to me through studying and meditating Rudolf Steiners 'Philosophy of Freedom'. After this first book I wrote many others, including novels about the same theme. Many of them have been translated into German. And perhaps many *will* be also appear in English...

Mieke Mosmuller, Baarle Nassau, March 2012.

PREFACE OF THE FIRST DUTCH EDITION

To make the reading of this book simpler, I would like to make some comments about style and composition. Actually, there is only **one** fundamental idea at the base of this book; I needed many words to make this one idea perceptible. Language has put many difficulties in the way, because I am aware that readers initially only have *words* with which to grasp this idea that is itself expressed in words. Actually, the book is not so much about language as about ideas, which are embodied in language. I would therefore like to justify the particular way I have used language in this book. I have not been consistent in using modern spelling, because in particular words, to my way of thinking, the living concept is better expressed by maintaining the old spelling; in other words, modern spelling has become generalised to the point where absolute compliance with certain rules would make the text unreadable. For example, in one sentence we have the word 'abstract' next to the word 'concrete'. Secondly, I have used 'he' and 'we' interchangeably, but I have never used 'she'. I have used 'I' as far as possible when I wanted to express inner, solitary experiences. I have used 'we' when I want to summon 'us' to activity. In descriptions I have occasionally used 'man' or 'he'. I have used 'he' deliberately, because this work is about the realisation of the 'self' as individuality. This is a realisation that comes about independently of gender. Therefore, although a 'she' myself, I have not felt the need to give prominence to this being a 'she'. An individuality does not have to feel less – nor more – than another person, because he is strong within himself and has room for others because of that.

Concerning the composition of the book, I have to say the following: the prologue and the epilogue should be considered as belonging to the main work. One can not rightly evaluate the core of this work, which arises out of *philosophia*, knowledge, love and contemplation, if one omits the prologue and epilogue. The work seeks to be an image of the organism of *living* thinking. As a plant cannot grow without its roots, nor can it form seed without flowering, organic thinking cannot live when it has to think in fragments. What is developed as an inner position in the prologue, so as to be able to posit the first question, is transformed in the epilogue into a position that seems to be like the first, but which can only be accepted as true *after* the path that lies between them has been travelled.

Mieke Mosmuller, The Hague, September 1994

PROLOGUE

PHILOSOPHY OR RELIGION?

He who has science and art
Also has religion,
He who has neither of these two,
Let him have religion

J. W. von Goethe,

Zahme Xenien VI.

In philosophy man struggles with the help of his thinking for an understanding of the riddles of existence, of his own existence and of the existence of the world, and for the capacities to penetrate himself and the world with concepts. He does not want to presuppose any truths and develop further thoughts from these presupposed truths – axioms – but rather, he wants to link concepts with one another through pure thinking, going forward from one concept to the next without leaps of thought which would weaken the argumentation.

Through a cohesive system of concepts, the philosopher seeks to show the truth of his thinking, which renders any further discussion unnecessary or impossible. The quality of his argumentation confirms the truth of its propositions. Thus, ideally, a system of concepts would be developed that would be completely self-contained, a system that rested in itself and that proved itself through its 'harmonious unity'.

In such a system of concepts there would not be a single, unclear, unconsidered point. There is an inner connection between all the concepts; there are no clashing or isolated concepts. Harmony in the thinking prevails; it is a harmony of spheres. Consciously or not, the philosopher holds such pure thinking to be his ideal.

He has to struggle within himself against disorder and rigidity in the concepts in his thinking. On the one hand, he finds in his thinking a series of lifeless concepts, and on the other, he requires an inner lawfulness and relationship between concepts because he yearns for this composed, harmonious, provable, pure organism of concepts.

There must, then, consciously or unconsciously – live in the philosopher the inner conviction that this ideal is achievable, or at least, he must have the *hope* that this is a true ideal. If he wished to apply his philosophy only as a means of proving that this ideal can never be realised, he would nevertheless have to have confidence in his argumentation. Thereby, however, his own aim – namely, to provide proof that an argument can never be cohesive - would be undermined. Hence, the philosopher always seeks after a true organism that is self-supporting and cohesive – but not closed! Were he to find this, then he would also have harmonised and purified his own thinking - for he himself is the thinker.

In our time this may appear to be a naive point of view, but whoever seriously asks himself what philosophers are striving to do and who confronts himself in an unprejudiced manner, will have to admit that either thinking can be trusted and that philosophy makes sense, or that thinking is but a dubious show and that philosophy is therefore absurd.

We have noticed in the 20th century – though the origins of this development lie much earlier – how philosophy has increasingly become merely a science among the other sciences and how it has lost its own character, which is actually to be the bearer of the other sciences. Philosophy has become more and more an abstract science, separated from its own reality, which is thinking. The philosophical thought content has become scientific thinking, exact and specialised, but has steadily separated itself from its own reality, where it has its origins and which is its instrument, namely, thinking itself. The danger arises thereby that one certainly develops an increasing exactness in the way thoughts are dealt with, but that through the enormous growth of the thought *content*, of the number of concepts, the possibility of an overview of concepts, and of spherical harmony between all concepts is lost. One thinks in long, exact sequences of concepts, which can be extended almost indefinitely. These sequences stand by themselves and are self-referential; they do not easily enable connections to be made between them.

Abstraction is *necessary* in thinking, because one wants to move freely in thinking, moved by nothing other than the inner lawfulness (logic) of the concepts themselves. However, there is the danger that one pushes this abstraction too far, whereby one can even lose the knowledge of this lawfulness, as the concepts are more and more experienced as lifeless marionettes that can be moved around arbitrarily, as the thinker pleases.

This separation between, on the one hand, the content of thinking, and on the other hand, the *knowledge* of the lawfulness of the *form* that bears thinking, has led to

17

religion becoming an increasingly isolated stream in the life of human culture. Goethe's words remain true: "He who has science and art, also has religion." In the twentieth century we have seen a divide open up between the science of sciences (philosophy) and religion.

The original philosophical ideal, which is a metaphysical ideal, namely, the discovery of a thinking that is self-supporting, sound, harmonious, and organic, is ultimately also a deeply religious ideal. One trusts that thinking is to be trusted. One has not then simply become a believer, so that one can believe in God, but one knows that there is *something* in life which one can trust, namely the value of thinking. This metaphysical side of philosophy has been quite lost in the twentieth century, it has been entirely excised.

By contrast, theology, although a knowledge of religion, is still not religion itself. Theology still has belief as a goal of enquiry, as a theme of research. One can very well at the same time be both an atheist and yet a theologian.

In our scientific age, faith is not a quality of thinking (any longer), we have to search for it in other areas of human experience.

The yearning for security, for reunion with a divine origin, for support, spills from the emotional life onto the beach of the life of thought. Certain facts in the development of the world and religious doctrines that result from them (those of Buddha, of Christ) come to a stop in the life of thoughts. This thinking is then not the self-supporting organism of pure thinking, but is borne by yearnings, which are rooted in the life of feeling and will, and not in thinking itself.

One becomes a believing person through yearnings, and

18

these yearnings indeed lead to thinking but they are rightly set aside by the scientist or the philosopher as unscientific, because he is bound to consider this religious thought content as a 'falling back below the modern scientific level of cognition'. Religious thought contents lead him back to premises which have their origin in the emotional life, and it is precisely this kind of thought content that makes it impossible for him to develop an un-preconditioned, self-sustaining thinking.

This has led to the situation in which modern science does not allow any ideals to be its driving forces. An ideal is always an idea carried by feeling and desire. Whoever wants to bring an ideal into science – and therefore also into the science of sciences (philosophy) bases this science on the life of feeling and will and bases it therefore on a subjective element, causing it to fall below the level of objective scientific cognition. There we have a problem, for we are asserting that there *is* a philosophical ideal.

The yearning of philosophy – which is also there in the word philosophy itself – for a reliable thinking, for a science of sciences, for *wisdom*, must only stimulate the philosopher to the *activity* of thinking; it must not determine *the content of his thinking*. The pure meaning of the word 'philosophy' already carries this driving, stimulating, yearning ideal within itself. When one allows oneself to be stimulated to scientific research by will and feeling, one does not carry into one's thinking any subjective element but rather an objective force which does not push the thinking below a scientific level but *lifts it beyond itself*. In this regard, philosophy also has religion.

Whoever, therefore, in philosophising, has an ideal and

is conscious of it seeks to provide proof that one can trust thinking. In proving this, he himself overcomes his doubt in thinking; he overcomes doubt as a phenomenon. This doubt, which expresses itself in abstract thinking is reshaped into a self-confident, self-critical trust, into a faith through self-confident knowledge.

In earlier centuries there was still knowledge of this task of philosophy and of its religious ideal. Joseph Haydn composed an opera, *Orpheus and Eurydice*, which had the subtitle 'Il anima del filosofo' (The Soul of Philosophy). After the death of his beloved Eurydice, Orpheus is advised to become a philosopher and is thus able to enter the realm of the dead.

Our present rationality regards these images as childish dreaming, but if one were to take them seriously, one might find in them much creative wisdom that works out of reality.

When, on the other hand, one looks at the meaning of the word 'religion' in its purest meaning, one finds that it points to a re-uniting. It is also in this sense that one can call the task of the philosophy religious. For when one can reconnect abstract thinking – which is a thinking that has become detached from one's own self - with one's own self again, one brings about a reunification. One makes religion literally true.

This book wishes to be a philosophical work: it ventures to make an attempt to find that point in thinking itself - which is both the instrument and at the same time the working area of the philosopher - where doubt has its origin.

We want to make this attempt, proceeding from the ideal

of the philosopher: we do not want to make use of any kind of prior knowledge that lies outside of thinking, or introduce any premises, but rather, to seek to conduct a self-enclosed yet free argumentation in which, as far as possible, there is not one single unresolved point which weakens the argument or makes it dubious. We want to shed light on doubt as a phenomenon and show how this doubt *must* make room for faith, for faith as a phenomenon – for that faith in self-aware knowledge, in the moment when thinking recognises itself.

Therefore this work is also a religious work, because it wishes to *prove* that the human being is united with a reality and that the becoming aware of this union is a re-uniting and thus, religion is.

PHILOSOPHY AS WONDERMENT

Joyously, so long ago,
My eager mind did strive
To study and discover
Nature in her works alive:
She, the everlasting Oneness
In the manyness divined.
Big minuteness, tiny bigness,
All according to its kind,
Ever changing, ever constant
Near and far, far and near,
Shaping and reshaping . . .
Why but to wonder am I here!

J.W. von Goethe - Parabase.

Goethe gives evidence in this poem of a true natural scientific method of research. But philosophy too takes its start from wonderment. One must be able to enquire out of wonderment. He who already knows everything does not need philosophy, just as little as he who sleeps through life. However, he who experiences something in life, even the smallest something, as a mystery, is inherently a philosopher. To be able to solve a riddle, one needs wonder. One wonders when one does *not* know something, when one has the courage to be interested and to admit to oneself: 'I don't know.' Really good questions spring from wonderment. What one *knows*, or an answer to a question, prompts not wonderment but satisfaction or gratitude.

Questioning arises from wondering, and one must be able to 'forget' what one already knows: Firstly, one must be able to forget the content of what one knows, because otherwise, this content would influence one's questioning and thereby distort the question that arises. Secondly, in true questioning one must put aside the attitude of one who knows, because this knowing attitude would darken the light which the question in its entire scope and all its aspects causes to appear. However, one may keep that which one has *become* through learning, cognition, and knowing. Through the act of knowing, one is a human being in the process of becoming. Before I had started my medical studies, I was a completely different person from who I was after I finished my medical studies. Of course I changed in that period because of the life lessons I experienced, but also through the knowledge I gained. And when now, in philosophising, I can leave all my knowledge out of consideration and at the same time still be able to realize that all my knowing is not yet wisdom, then I can understand *myself* as someone who is in the process of becoming when I am philosophising. Yes, this person who *I am* is the starting point for asking in wonderment.

Fear of the unknown, of the not yet known, of the 'I do not know it (yet)' on the one hand, and the self-satisfaction of 'I already know that', through what is familiar, what is understood on the other hand, are the two enemies of wonder. These two strive against any questioning.

But can one ask capriciously? Can one start asking questions at any point one pleases? Can one ask: what is the human being, what is thinking, what is being, what is logic, etc.? Are answers at all *possible* here?

Or is there a prior question, a question which really can only be posed first? Is it possible to find this first question and indeed, in such a way that the answer to it will organically call up a new question?

23

Philosophy is not a game of chess, in which at the beginning, all the concepts are already in a certain order. The first chess move in a certain sense determines the whole game. Every move defines the course of the game more strictly, until a checkmate ends the process.

At the beginning of philosophising, no fixed position of concepts can already serve as a starting point; inwardly, one must hold oneself quite impartially without being a fool. For it would be foolishness if one were not to discover a *specific* question, if one wanted to remain in one's impartiality. The first question I have found determines the course of my philosophy. If I can choose my first question freely without any kind of inner necessity through lawfulness in thinking itself, then my question does not well up from wonderment, but from partiality, subjective partiality. Through my inclination I choose a first question from various possible questions and I *call* this question the first question.

However, If I leave all my opinions, preferences, and knowledge out of consideration, if I only observe the riddle of where to start in my questioning, then a question becomes visible which lies even before the first question, namely: with which question does a philosophy begin in wonderment?

THE ART OF ASKING

'Thus it happened because of the sin
that You have loaded upon Yourself,
that thou did not ask for the lance and
the Grail
and because of that, many other bad
things
have happened to You.'

Parsival – Chrestien de Troyes.

Before we can give this first question a concrete content,
we should submit the questioning itself to examination. In
this prologue we do not yet apply an exact technique of
logical thinking, but we develop free, naïve observation.
When I inwardly observe myself as a human being questioning, I can know directly from this observation, from
this inner perceiving, that this questioning on my part
signifies that I am in a state of unknowing. This can be
a general questioning. I can be conscious that a human
being has a limited knowledge, that he does *not* know
many things, that he is actually always unsatisfied because
of that, and that as a human being, he is always striving.
He is always striving for a more complete knowledge.

I have a concrete question on the other hand, when I
become aware that my knowing is incomplete, when I
confirm that I lack specific knowledge. I inwardly clothe this
lack in words and experience the yearning to find an answer.

Questioning flows from imperfection. The experience of a question for which no answer has yet been found stimulates our awareness of our human inadequacy. Man does not like feeling inadequate, and this is why most questioning goes on unconsciously.

Through their upbringing and through our own actions, children are driven out of the paradise of not-knowing as soon as possible. We try to make them stuff themselves earlier and earlier from the tree of knowledge. They get so much information - at an age in which questioning is a life need – that nothing is left over for them to ask about; there is nothing for them to wish for. And when a child is still not satisfied by all the knowledge it gets, when there is no end to its questions and it is highly intelligent then it has to jump a class or two at school. For questions *must* certainly be answered, and preferably before they are even asked.

If modern education achieves one sure result, it is to wean the child away from its natural inclination to question. The child develops a passive, non-critical mode of learning and is taught to be a student who can complete a course of study at university within a few years, quickly, efficiently, based almost entirely on factual knowledge: much knowledge but few questions.

But *life* is also our teacher and life presents riddles to every human being. Love and suffering do not bring man scientific questions but life questions and in doing so, they protect the human capacity to question. However, this book does not concern itself with this questioning attitude to life, but with how to regain a questioning attitude in *science*.

When we therefore begin to search for a first question,

are we trying to take a 'standpoint', from which we can begin, without already assuming a *knowing*? Do we search for a standpoint in which we ourselves consist entirely of 'question'? Or can specific knowledge be the starting point, from where we can begin with our questioning and feel our way forward step by step in our questioning, without prejudice and without assumptions? Is there a knowing which does not belong to assumptions? In the first case, I empty my consciousness entirely of content; it is just a form, without any content whatsoever. I myself live in this empty consciousness, questioning. In the second case, in the moment that I see a concrete question appear in my mind, arbitrariness enters the activity of my thinking. I must therefore recognize how I, as a questioner without questions, am condemned to exist forever in nothingness; I can take no step without falling into capriciousness. I must return to the state of complete questioning and will never be able to make a start from my thinking.

Although it is not so easy to realise this inner state – this is the striving of the Buddhist and the mystic – and many readers will only be able to *imagine* this inner condition, it will nevertheless be clear that in this state, one would have to refrain from the possibility of philosophising. These experiences, which the mystics describe, for example, Nicholas of Cusa in his *De Docta Ignorantia* (Of Learned Ignorance) may perhaps turn out to be the result of a true philosophy; it cannot be the starting point of one.

Is it possible then to find a point in consciousness from which the first question springs *directly*, and so not through a choice that *I* make? Is there a certain content in my consciousness that I can keep when I begin questioning,

27

without mixing my *own* will, my capriciousness, in with the philosophy? Is philosophising subject to spiritual laws – as natural science is subject to laws of nature – and am I able to recognize these laws and to follow them, not in accordance with *my* will, but in accordance with the spirit of the thing itself? Can I ask the first question with certainty, sure that there is no prior question? Can I be so sure in my finding of this first question that I no longer need to doubt it?

Or is doubt a necessary human characteristic which one has to accept and which one ought not even to *want* to overcome? What would man be if he no longer doubted? Would we then not also take from him the possibility of belief?

THE BENEFIT OF THE DOUBT

One could possibly imagine that there is something compulsive about the philosopher's search for a first question. Perhaps it is an exaggerated conscientiousness, a demand which he can never fulfill. The human being can have a deep-rooted conviction that he can never know anything with complete certainty: that being human means living with probabilities, which at every moment must be revised by new facts. When one feels oneself a human being in this sense, then one cannot trust thinking; it is only a game with concepts. Who is the master in this game? Who is the most intelligent? I can argue ever more cleverly, but one will try to see through my argumentation and detect illogical thought constructs. A professor of philosophical anthropology (Patricia de Martelaere) formulated this as follows in an interview with a Dutch newspaper (NRC Handelsblad): 'Philosophy is something between science and nonsense. Science has a more philosophical nature than it seems to have at first sight. Can the scientific researcher ever be objective, can he ever reach certainty? From this viewpoint science is philosophy. But philosophy is not totally absurd. It has something of science-fiction, but then literally: science and fiction at the same time. Fantastic presentations which outsiders regard as nonsensical. But it is enjoyable to think something up and one never knows whether it is correct.'

Seriousness, as the basic attitude of the philosopher, is not the hallmark of such a statement. Someone who thinks that philosophising is a necessity in life, work in which one has to search for certainty in one's questions and answers, will feel that in making such a statement he is mocked as being 'much too serious.'

Another way of thinking in probabilities is the philosophy of George Moore. He considers the thesis that the probability that something is true increases with the *number* of people that considers it to be true. Many people consider a great deal to be true without the need of philosophy to prove it. George Moore calls this 'common sense'. In his view, if one is to philosophise, it is above all important that, with the help of language, the questions be formulated as clearly as possible so that they can only be understood in a single way; this gives the best opportunity for a right answer. For George Moore it is not the 'what' but the 'how' in one's questioning that is important. The search for a first question thus loses its meaning, for it is not then a matter of which question is the first question but rather, that every question one asks be correctly and unambiguously formulated. Seen in this way, thinking becomes an amorphous mass which we can engage with at any arbitrary point in order to illuminate something, as long as we formulate our questions clearly.

Both of these philosophers thus show that they believe that thinking itself is not to be trusted and that there is no guarantee for truth in it. Thinking is fiction as soon as it leaves worldly reality; how far it is reliable when it is controlled by a reality that lies outside thinking itself is a scientific, philosophical question.

One can also think out a logic that is completely removed from thinking and is extended in space: speech is an image of such a logic extended in space; thinking is an internalised speech. Ludwig Wittgenstein:[1] „Die Tatsachen im logischen Raum sind die Welt" (The facts in logical space are the world). „Jedes Ding ist, gleichsam, in einem Raume möglicher Sachverhalte. Diesen Raum kann ich mir leer denken, *nicht aber das Ding ohne den Raum."* (Every thing is at the same time in a space of possible facts. I can think of this space as empty *but I cannot think of the thing without the space.*)

Philosophers write clever, elaborate works that are often hard to understand and thus they become university professors. One cannot simply assert that all or much of what they say is nonsense. When we seek to find trust in thinking, we must also be clear as to how we relate to the thinking of others. Can we trust our thinking? Do we indeed want to trust it? Or is it more of an advantage for us to doubt? Doubt rules modern thinking. It is the sovereign in the realm of thinking. Why is this sovereign able to maintain his rulership? Do we ourselves recognize him as king because he sits on his throne as a righteous ruler? Or is he a dictator?

Doubt has three faces. It lives in us as an inner ease as intellectual compulsion or as insecurity, which, when we bear it patiently, turns into insight. Inner comfort and intellectual compulsion are the masks behind which doubt hides itself as a dictator.

The true, honest face of doubt is a patient concern; this is the pure doubt, doubt in its right place.

31

Doubt as ease.

Whoever doubts does not have to commit himself to anything or anyone. When I say 'yes' or 'no', I bind myself and have to hold to my judgment. I have to be constant and face up to the problems that result from my yes or no. When I make a choice and do not doubt its correctness and validity, I am bound to this choice as a result. When I doubt my ideas, I do not have to make them my ideals. Every step I take is accompanied by the possible excuse: 'to err is human'.

Doubt as intellectual compulsion.

Every result of abstract thinking can be doubted. When one thinks, consciously or not, that thinking is a reflection of reality in word and image, when it is seen as identical to the imaginative life, which is coloured by the subject who is thinking, it can never be trusted fully; the result of this thinking must always be doubted.

On the one hand, my thinking is always imperfect, because I will never have in my life a complete reflection of the whole reality of the world. On the other hand, there is always the danger that my thinking will become impure in that my own subjective opinions and judgments transform my thinking into *my personal image of the world*.

Tomorrow it can turn out that I will have to change my imaginations in order to come a little closer to reality. A full merging of the worlds of imagination and reality will, however, never be achieved; we have an endless journey to make.

This form of doubt has in our time become the scientific attitude. Whoever thinks he can know something with full certainty is regarded as an unscientific fool or a fanatic. Jürgen Habermas writes in *Post-Metaphysical thougt*:[2]

'Finally, the methodically cultivated cognition of modern sciences loses its own autarchy. Thinking, in that it engages with the whole of nature and history, which functions in both an all-encompassing and self-reflecting manner, was obliged to ground itself in, and identify itself as, philosophical knowledge – either through arguments on ultimate foundations, or through spiral-shaped self-explications of comprehensive concepts. The premises on which scientific theories are based, on the other hand, are considered to be hypotheses and must be confirmed by consequences – either through empirical confirmation, or through coherence with other, already accepted statements. *The falsifiability of scientific theories is incompatible with the form of cognition in which the prima philosophica had confidence* (italicisation by author). Every comprehensive, coherent and definitive system of statements should be formulated in a language that requires no commentary and no longer allows for any aloof interpretation, correction or innovation; it should bring the record of its own activity to a halt. This sealing-off character is incompatible with the unprejudiced openness of the development of scientific knowledge.'

In this quotation one finds the bold statement that unprejudiced openness (impartiality, objectivity) would be in contradiction to the discovery of truth, which one no longer needs to refute or is able to refute. A certain opposition is set up here. On the one hand, there is the view of the old (classical) philosophy that thinking has its own reality with its own lawfulness that is either carried into life on earth from out of a world of Ideas (Plato) or discovered through contact with the earthly world and its lawfulness (Aristotle) - in both cases essential truths are to be found. On the other hand, there is the view of modern (natural) science that thinking has to follow reality and derives its right to exist from that but that it has to be corrected by empirical facts over and over again in a never-ending process of searching for truth and doubting the facts that are discovered.

Whether this contradiction really exists or not is one of the questions which will be answered in this book. If the contradiction does exist, then science is condemned to a state of restlessness which will never come to an end.

Doubt as patience.

Doubt, however, has a meaning. As a phenomenon in the inner life of the human being, it is a 'benefit'. It is a process that, if it can be endured, leads to insight.

Every human being must make decisions in his life. And every human being has experienced doubt when it comes to making the right choice. One cannot always have a feeling of certainty about the rightness of the decisions one has to make. One is in doubt. Whoever has the courage to *endure* this doubt for a while, to look it in the eye so to speak, who in the meantime energetically researches the different possibilities and lets them work upon himself for a while, will notice after a while that the doubt transforms into insight. The time needed for this can vary and depends, amongst other things, on the weight of the decision to be taken. Doubt is thus a justified phase in the process of decision, and gives way to the insight, in what to do.

An important distinction between the different forms of doubt arises through the relationship to the point in time at which doubt appears in the process of decision.

When it is the doubt that arises from a desire for ease or comfort, doubt accompanies the whole process of decision-making and remains after the choice has been made. Thus no real choice is made at all.

Doubt as intellectual compulsion is an intrinsic symptom of abstract intellectual thinking. When I, as a scientist, re-gard my thinking as a subjective accompaniment to reality, I must struggle constantly to direct my thinking to reality. My hypotheses might always be my own fantasies without me being aware of it; I constantly have to test them against reality and against the results of others' research in order to make them conform to these if necessary. The posing of a hypothesis is ruled by doubt and likewise, the results of my scientific work. Doubt is an unavoidable phenomenon here. Were I not in my abstract thinking to be doubting constantly, I would be ensnared in self-deception.

Doubt as patience, however, always precedes the making of choices. Doubt works here as patience, as an honest not-knowing, as awareness of having a question to which the answer is not *yet* clear. Whoever has the courage to endure this doubt sooner or later experiences a moment in which it metamorphoses itself into a certainty about what has to be done and how. This is the pure human form of doubt, which accompanies every human life and every decision. Through this form of doubt man realizes that he is *free*, that his actions are not predetermined, and that there is as much to be said for this or that choice. That man has freedom in this doubt also follows from his abstract thinking, for in such thinking he does not experience himself to be in touch with reality. But if he is patient and takes his time, life itself will become his teacher in his thinking and show him what is good. This is the effect of *life*. Life itself metamorphoses doubt into certainty, but then takes from man his direct feeling of freedom. Here there is a field of tension: freedom lives in doubt. Is there also freedom in certainty? Can I recreate the link between thinking and reality so that reality *in* thinking overcomes doubt, while fully maintaining freedom in thinking? And how does certainty relate to belief? Someone who has no certainty must rely on belief. In doubt lies the possibility of belief; is there also belief in certainty? Out of this field of tension again arises the matter of the first question. How does this first question sound, this question which is put to me by reality, in such a way that I do not need to ask if this is really the first question?

How does this question - which only *I* can ask with my thinking – sound in such a way that I am not subject to the dictates of reality and can retain my freedom? Stated like this, the question seems to lead to an impasse. The tension of this (apparent) impasse will continue through the next chapter. It cannot be set aside with only a few words. To approach the question we must first learn to take an objective look at ourselves.

We must practice self-knowledge.

O MAN, KNOW YOURSELF!

If I know my relationship
To myself and to the outer world
I call it truth.
And so can every man have his own truth
And yet it is always the same

J.W. von Goethe, Sprüche in Prosa, Das
Erkennen.
(Verses in Prose, Knowing)

In this first verse from the 'Sprüche in Prosa' (Verses in Prose), Goethe evinces directly his view that truth does not only mean conformity with the facts, but that self-knowledge plays a mediating role in finding the truth. Knowledge is not only a matter of penetrating the outer world with concepts, but I must understand first, how I relate to myself and second, how I relate to the outer world.

This verse is not cited here because we want to acknowledge or reject it. But we do want to follow the call for self-knowledge and observe in advance that there are various forms of self-knowledge. If we want to posit the concept of self-knowledge plausibly, we must proceed in a manner that is both extensive and exact.
First, we can make a rough distinction between observing the outer world and observing our own self. But when we consider the matter more closely, it will

37

turn out that both worlds are intimately interwoven.

Observing the outer world

We perceive the outer world through our senses. But do our senses perceive only the outer world? Here we come across the first intertwinement, because with our senses, we also observe our own body. Many people in our time feel this body as the 'self'. When I stand in front of the mirror I see 'myself'; I see 'myself' in the outer world. This is a purely external perception of my I. I have a direct, unmirrored perception of this 'self' when I look at my body, touch it etc. I can never see my own face, but I can see certain body parts. I thus have a direct impression of my corporeal self in the external sense.

Besides this I can have an *inner* observation of my body. I experience my body as mine and from the inside of this body with help from the senses that have their field of observation in the body itself I experience fatigue, fever, balance,   tension in the muscles etc. Is this experience an inner experience, or should I call it an inner sensory perception? When I have attached the experience of my I exclusively to my corporeal existence, then I will indeed experience this field of observation as *inner* experience, but my inner experiences are not limited to the experience of my body.

Besides the experience of my own body as the knowledge of my I, anatomy and psychology also belong to the area of self-knowledge. Certainly, this has to do with so-called scientific self-knowledge, for it concerns not only *my own* body but all human bodies, yet it is still a part of the human

I. Despite this, a student of the medical sciences will not easily *experience* his studies as a path of self-knowledge. Unprejudiced observation leads to the following insight: during my life my body belongs to the outer world as well as to my I. It belongs to the outer world as far as it is a part of the whole of nature. My I nevertheless raises it from the general, outer world and gives it its individual shape and function during my life; it makes it into an individual instrument. Through death the body returns to the general natural processes and becomes completely a part of the outer world.

The observation of my body gives me a double experience: on the one hand, through my body I am just an example of the human species, which belongs to the kingdoms of nature. On the other hand, I experience through my body my being different from other human beings. Like you, I have a heart, a liver, two lungs. But my face is different from yours, and so are the growth pattern of my hair, my shape, my facial expressions, my way of moving etc. I can of course conclude that this being different is genetically determined and thus has its roots in a natural process, but it is nevertheless something remarkable in nature that there are so many differences between human beings which cannot be found within any species of animals. Within the human species there is a further differentiation which makes of every human being an individuality. When one truly thinks this through to the end, one can never conclude that this individuation is *exclusively* of genetic origin: that would imply the existence of a linear, continuously bifurcating movement, by which we would be dragged along. Our I would arise from this whirling stream, but we would never be able to become aware of it. The human being indeed receives his body from nature but within this nature of his a creative artist is at work, who moulds his instrument, the body, so that the I, the individual human being, is able to become the master of its body. Man makes a work of art out of his life.

Observation of the spirit (inner self-observation)

When we then pass over to an observation of our inner, non-physical life, we must direct our perception not to our body but to our consciousness. We have already shown so-called inner experiences as perceptions of an outer world. If we therefore here speak of inner observation, we always mean the purely inner observation of our consciousness. That the human being can turn his gaze towards his inner experience is a specifically human capacity. It is given to us as a possibility by nature, but its development depends on practice. When we practise observing our consciousness, it becomes all the more exact and intensive. Whoever reads these lines should actually not want to read further without himself attempting this observation of his own consciousness. Then he could experience for himself what is being written about here. Whoever does not want to make this step towards his own activity will find this book boring and will perhaps not notice his own indolence.

One can thus from now on certainly remain in one's comfortable chair, but one will have to bestir oneself inwardly and want to stand up, otherwise one will not find much satisfaction in this work and will not experience the effect of the book. It is not a matter of giving a description of the results of observation of the mind; the point is to carry out this observation itself while reading. Thus we turn our gaze inwards, and the first thing we encounter there is our mental images.

We meet a great wealth of mental images which clothe themselves in inner spoken words and pictures which, when we do not exert ourselves, string themselves together naturally and give us an image of ourselves and of our being merged together with the world. This view of our thought life clearly shows us at first sight that we can indeed close our senses to the world – we can close our eyes, seek silence from the outer world etc. but that our mind is nevertheless filled with remembrances of the outer world, is even *exclusively* filled with them. We observe a colourful miscellany of memory pictures, items of knowledge, mental images related to intentions, our sensations and feelings, our wishes etc. At first, our consciousness is filled with mental images, not with feelings or with deeds, but with mental images of feelings and deeds. All these mental images, these mental representations live in pictures derived from the outer world. I myself live in these images actively or passively; *I* am the one who brings something about in these images, experiences something, remembers something, everything relates to my I, while I experience at the same time that the mental images string themselves together outside my will. Is it human destiny that we must always keep on riding such a carousel at this colourful fair?

Our emotional life reveals itself in our consciousness less directly than the display of our mental images. Behind the mask of images of feeling such as 'I am sad', 'I am happy' live feelings themselves as forces which are far more real than the mental images. Feelings are naturally awakened by something outside myself or inside myself. I translate them into mental images in order to explain them, but I *experience* them directly as forces. These *forces* can even have a direct physical effect: for example, warmth due to happiness, or cold due to sorrow. Feelings bring me as subject into a relationship with the objective world; they determine my personal relationship to it. Feelings, therefore, are forces which are experienced as more real than thoughts, but they lie deeper in consciousness and their meaning only becomes clear when they have clothed themselves in a mental image. Yet through this mental representation they lose their real character.

Whenever we wish to be active, we must engage with our *will*. Whether this action comes about through a personal wish or through a command makes no difference for the nature of willing. When we talk about *willing* here, we mean becoming active. Willing is force in an even greater measure than feeling. The force of willing condenses itself here to *my* being, which I call ´I´. I experience every act as my own particular activity. *I* myself must stir my body to activity, even if it is against my will, if I am forced to work. The result of the activity is always *my* work.

In my willing I live as 'I', I experience the reality of my being. Nothing comes into being if *I* do not become active. Yet it is particularly this area of my being, namely, my will, that lies the most deeply hidden within my consciousness. The results of my willing are concrete, reality, tangible. The willing itself I sleep through completely. I cannot

42

consciously follow how the willing comes about. The *mental images* of what I want and what I have to do live in my consciousness. There too live the mental images of the feelings which the will does or does not support. But the essential power of the will escapes me entirely.

My human powerlessness is characterized by these three areas in consciousness: What I know consciously – thinking - I cannot do. What I do or how I do it – willing – evades my consciousness. Between these two poles live my changing joys and sorrows.

Man can free himself from this powerlessness. In the Bhagavad Gita we find the following lines:[3]

"The senses are great;
The intellect shows itself to be greater,
"Reason" is yet greater still,
But above all these stands the spirit".

Liberation from the above-mentioned powerlessness commences at the moment when we realize that we have only observed the *content* of consciousness, which is immediately and concretely present. We direct our view inwards and observe what lives in our consciousness as that given *content* which has not arisen through our own activity. Then we 'see' our powerlessness, our lack of freedom. Nevertheless, when we observe in this way, the *activity* itself always escapes our attention, for the attention – the inner attention – is directed at the observation of the consciousness. It observes that upon which we direct it.

43

But the activity itself, the directing of the attention *itself*, the inner observation, the *observer himself*, escapes the observation.

In order to discover this active content of our consciousness, we must take an extra step and direct our attention to the observer himself, thus to our own activity in our inner observing. When we really try to take this step, we will experience an indescribable feeling of powerlessness, because now we are asked to release our inner capacity of observation from the passive content in order to be able to guide it towards the *process* of self-observation. This form of self-observation is *not* given to us naturally; we have to want to develop it ourselves. One can live one's life and die without *ever* having resorted to this self-observation. One does not have to take this step, and yet it is a step which is necessary, if one really wants to know what human powerlessness is. One finds one's own human nature when one finds oneself in one's own, fully conscious inner activity.

One sees how one is always going on with the intellect, which always escapes the attention when one does not begin to observe one's activity not only outwardly but also inwardly. But the unusualness of this inner observation causes one to realise one's own powerlessness in its most extreme form. It is in this very powerlessness, however, that one finds the possibility to awaken and to stand upright. Thus one is led from observation with the senses to the intellect – the observation of the content of consciousness occurs through the intellect - and from the intellect (*Verstand*) to the reason (*Vernunft*), for the observation

44

of the process of thinking occurs through one's reason. Through this entire process, what one really finds is finally the Spirit:

"The senses are great;
The intellect shows itself to be greater,
"Reason" is yet greater still,
But above all these stands the spirit".

One finds the Spirit in the way it reveals itself in its first form, namely, in the form of the primal human spiritual activity, in the appearance of one's own spiritual being. This being accompanies all the activity of consciousness, but escapes observation, as an 'open secret'.

Nevertheless, we must repeat that this form of self-knowledge is not given to us naturally. Practising it will at first lead to feelings of powerlessness, because during this life on earth our Spirit must *learn* to observe itself. And this learning can not – as can *all* other learning processes – be achieved without the deepest experience. This learning calls for our whole spiritual being. And because we are used to abstract learning, which only calls upon our heads, and not to learning with our full human being, we feel powerless. We lack the power to realise this 'O Man, Know Yourself.' And in this powerlessness we hear directly the inner voice which says: 'this is impossible, stop it, it is nonsense, it is not scientific, etc.'

However, whoever is willing to try over and over again, to bear the powerlessness that arises when we tear our self-observation loose from the content of the mind and direct it at the observation itself; whoever rouses his *will* to start this new learning process intentionally in order to experience the spirit with his spirit, he experiences the transformation of powerlessness into *freedom*.

He experiences the moment when he truly becomes a human being. He experiences that this observing of observation is at the same time a thinking about thinking. He finds the area where human thinking really *lives*, he experiences the source out of which all activity originates.

In this book I try to show the finding of this point of becoming human within thinking, through philosophy, and to prove that becoming human actually occurs at this point. That this is also a religious task may be clear from above-mentioned experience of the spirit through the spirit. One experiences the spirit in becoming free of the life of corporeal habits.

In the words of Meister Eckhart (On solitude)[4]:

'Here you should know that the Masters are speaking, that there are two kinds of human being in every human being: the one is called the outer man and this is the man of the senses; there are five senses that serve man, and he works through the power of the soul. The other man is called the inner man, and this is the inner life of man. Now you should know that every man who loves God no longer uses the powers of the soul that the outer man has when the five senses serve needs; and the inner life does *not* concern itself with the five senses, except only insofar as it is *the guide and conductor of the five senses* and protects them so that they do not indulge their striving towards animality.'

Now we have enough 'material' to put the first question, not because we have 'made up' this first question, but because it *is* the first question. With this first question, and the justification that this *is* the first question, we commence with the philosophical part of this work.

At the end of this prologue I want to draw to the reader's attention that all the 'material' from this prologue does not have any influence on the fundamental idea of the philosophy that will now follow. In the prologue I have described *how* one has to go about searching for the beginning of philosophy; the starting point that is eventually found is made possible by the character of this searching, but not influenced by it. In other words: what has been said in this prologue is not an answer to questions already posed before the first question and accepted as premises.

PHILOSOPHIA

INTRODUCTION

Philosophy is science, and science has to be objective.
Therefore philosophy has more and more come to belong
to the objective sciences on the one hand, or is directed
to the realm of thinking fantasy on the other. Thereby,
however, the original meaning and purpose of the concept
'philosophia' is lost. In this concept there are two human
capacities, which, when they fulfill each other *within* a
human being, make him into a philosopher. They are the
capacity of *love* and the capacity for *wisdom*.

In the present objective sciences neither of these two
human capacities has a place any longer. Love is seen as
something subjective; it is based on a personal preference
for one thing or the other, for the one or the other. Therefore
it must be kept out of the pursuit of science. My personal
preference would be to give the final results of science a
personal colour; this contradicts the scientific ideal.

Wisdom is a human capacity that is realised through
the course of life. When 'knowing' is lived through and
enriched by knowledge of life, then it is wisdom. It does not
have to be lived through only externally, a living through
of the things that happen in life, it can also be a living
through or working through that goes on purely inwardly.
But in both cases knowing *has gone through the personality*
and has thus lost its strictly objective character.

From this point of view there is no place for a true
philosophy among the objective sciences. This is factually
borne out in the disappearance of philosophy as an ancillary

51

subject alongside the exact sciences. We see philosophy appear more and more as a main subject, as an objective science in itself. Philosophy is no longer regarded as a necessary mode of reflection for every student and scientist in the way science is conducted, alongside the acquisition of factual scientific content, knowledge and skills. Even if the individual philosopher sees this differently, if he thinks that philosophy *does* have the task to summon the scientist (science) to self- reflection and self-knowledge, the *fact* still remains that students today learn *specialist subjects*, and that philosophical questions are not seen as belonging to these subjects. A true philosophia which seeks to awaken love and wisdom, the two human capacities that live in this word, would be able to achieve the synthesis between objective science and the individual human being who pursues that science, without subjectivising the science. But instead of being a mediator between man and science, philosophy has increasingly taken on a descriptive character. In philosophy too, the *quantity* of scientific material has become very large. One who comes from another specialism and seeks access to philosophy today – as for example in the case of the author - from a longing to take note of present thinking and a longing for reflection on the practice of one's own profession can get the feeling he is a naive fool who puts simplistic questions. Philosophical literature is immensely comprehensive, written in jargon, and seems at first to be a temple exclusively for insiders, a temple which can only be unlocked through academic philosophical study. Nevertheless, the alert student can notice that, by working through the introductory books, a certain *way* of studying and thinking is taught to him, which is already a *result* of the path philosophy has taken this century. The 'naive, foolish' open-mindedness is lost and one becomes a 'real' scientist. I, however, wanted to approach the great philosophical works with my naive open-mindedness intact and maybe I have forced the lock of the temple so that now a childish fool with simplistic questions has invaded the temple. These questions were asked a long time ago and are considered to have been answered and thus settled. Yet these questions should still be asked again: they should be asked in a different way and answered in a different way.

As philosophy – which springs from a true desire for contemplation – assumes a stronger objective character, with the result that it can no longer be experienced as fulfilling that desire for contemplation, this yearning searches for other paths on which to satisfy itself. For example, many people find these paths in the 'philosophies' of the New Age movement. In this movement many searching people find an answer to their questions, which rise to the surface with ever growing power. Those who follow these paths then leave the area of strictly objective sciences and give themselves over to impulses from other areas of the soul than those of thinking. Thinking then is often regarded as an abstract, cold area that must be eliminated in favor of the powers of love. The concept 'philosophy' loses its meaning because the two human capacities are divided from one another: one does not conduct his love to thinking, to the concepts anymore because in the world of concepts, one does find a world of wisdom but a region that is abstract, loveless, and cold. A disinclination to thinking comes about, and a disinclination to science, which is obtained with this thinking. One searches for the high road to wisdom on other paths than that of thinking.

A true Philosophia satisfies the desire of the scientist for clear, pure, objective thinking, as well as the common human need for an answer to life's questions which rise powerfully from the life of feeling and will.

PHILOSOPHIA

When, as is described in the Prologue, I direct my power of observation to my consciousness - to my full clear consciousness, thus to the area of my imaginative life - and I remove all concrete imaginative *content* from my consciousness, so that I do not make my knowledge, my life, my memories, indeed my personality to be the starting point of philosophy; when I wonder in astonishment in this imaginative emptiness how I have to start philosophising, then I experience the dilemma, the tension of the first question to be asked in its full strength. If I do not step out of this questioning in the mood of wonderment, if I do not ask a concrete question, I can never start philosophising. However, when I formulate a first question, this inevitably becomes *my* question, and perhaps *you* will have another question.

When I let this internal conflict truly sink in, when I can *experience* how there seems to be no way out; when I don't try to escape quickly from this conflict, but *dare* to experience this incapacity to solve it, then I slowly start to acknowledge, that this point of doubt (shall I ask or shall I hold back in not-questioning?) springs from primal fear, from the fear of transforming *myself*. I feel afraid to take this step, which is wholly mine. I have the full responsibility for this step. This fear is not a fear of this or that but fear itself as experience. It is my fear of giving birth to myself: I would like to escape from my responsibility and never emerge from it consciously.

However, when I remain stuck in questions that do not become concrete, I must give up on the philosophical ideal. As soon as I ask a concrete question, I give birth to *myself* in consciousness, and philosophy begins in a way that is totally mine. In this doubt which proceeds from fear – in relation to stepping back fully into the unborn All, into nothingness, *or* in giving birth to my own personality in this holy openness – the first question necessarily arises: If I want to come to the point of knowing, if I want to step out of this state of not-asking and not-knowing, in order to come to the point of knowing, then I will first have to understand knowing *itself*. The first question will have to be the question about knowledge itself and about the possibility of truth in knowing. Without this question and the answer to it, it is meaningless to embark on any philosophical, indeed on any scientific quest. Even the judgment that in moving from not-thinking to asking the first question, I ask a personal first question, *is already a judgment that is based on cognition*. I must get to know *the activating of thinking itself* if I am ever to know whether this has a subjective or objective character or is possibly something of a totally different order.

I must have the courage to initiate thinking, to give birth to myself from the silence of not-knowing and from the innocence of not-knowing. With the help of the power of observation which is directed at consciousness, I can then 'see' what takes place.

Or in more philosophically acceptable language:
Philosophy is not possible without the activation of thinking. When we observe our consciousness with our inner

eye, we find the content ready to hand; it has emerged of itself, without the onset of our own will activity; when we start philosophising, another element enters consciousness: we must *want* to start thinking.

Philosophy *is* thinking. However, how can man ever have trust in the truth of his philosophy if he does not know thinking through and through so that he *knows* what it means? The first question must therefore be the question about thinking itself.

If we do not know thinking itself, if we have not exactly cognized the transition from not-thinking to thinking activity, then we *do not* know our own role and its meaning for thinking and knowing. But in that case, we cannot make any statement about the subjective or objective character of thinking, neither do we know what the value of thinking is in understanding the world.

Here we find the primal moment of doubt: if I, as a human being, do not know exactly what the value is of human thinking, I am condemned to eternal doubt. To overcome this doubt, it is not enough to form hypotheses about, for example, the relation between thinking and truth. Doubt will only be finally overcome when in getting to know human thinking itself there is not the same insecurity as in knowing all other things. If we can not *know* with unassailable certainty what the value of thinking is, it becomes impossible to overcome doubt.

Alternately formulated: when the question about thinking takes on a scientific, theoretical character, the answer to the question will also be found theoretically. A theory comes about through thinking. In forming a theory of knowledge, a thinking about thinking, we undermine our theory theoretically. Or: if cognition can only be known in the same way as we cognize all other phenomena, we shall end up moving in a circle: the process of cognition can only be known through the process of cognition, which again we can only do with the help of thinking, etc.

Doubt can therefore only be overcome when there is a real difference between thinking about thinking, and thinking about everything else. Moreover, this difference must precisely be what gives us *certainty*. For in knowing everything other than thinking there is always doubt, because of the uncertainty about the value of thinking. Doubt *must* disappear when certainty is gained about the value of thinking about thinking, that is, the cognition of thinking, or epistemology.

It could be that after our research into the first question, we come to the conclusion that we can only approach thinking in the same way as everything else. Then thinking will remain, to use the Kantian expression, a 'thing-in-itself' (*Ding an sich*). In which case, we can not do other than declare everything else to be 'things in themselves' too. Then we have boundaries to our human knowledge and we have to be clear that nothing can be known with certainty.

Edmund Husserl says that truth is only possible when thinking can be judged according to a transcendental criterion, in other words, when thinking is not judged according to the same thinking that cognises everything else in human existence.

58

On the contrary, we say: there is another possibility. If thinking itself *substantially* differs from everything else that can be known, if there is an essential difference between the two, then the process of cognising (understanding) thinking itself will also be a substantially different process from that of cognising everything else. The cognitive process is not only determined by the way of thinking, but also by the being of the object that is to be cognised.

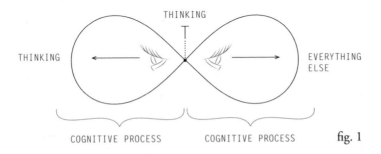

fig. 1

The eye of thinking looks outwards in cognising everything else; it looks inward in cognising thinking.

Thus we can not only escape from a never-ending regression, a moving in circles, by thinking about thinking in a different way (according to a transcendent criterion) from how we think about everything else, but also when we cognise - by means of *the same* thinking that we use to cognise everything else - that which is completely different from everything else, namely *thinking itself.*

Thinking and the instrument of cognition are the same thing, whereas the object of cognition of everything else is essentially different. In what follows, we want to show

59

that this difference between the being of thinking and the being of everything else is a fact, and that it is precisely this difference that determines certainty in thinking about thinking.

When, as with Edmund Husserl, we are of the view that thinking itself has to be judged according to a transcendent criterion if truth is to be found, this means that we have to apply a different thinking, a different knowing, in order to be able to judge thinking itself. However, this would mean that we must find this transcendent criterion first, and how else could we do that than again through thinking? Whatever statement or judgment we make always happens through thinking. The *fact* that we may not notice this, that we think that we experience certain judgments as automatically given, (call it intuition, pre-reflexive knowing, self-evident notions, etc.) does not matter and is based on an insufficiently precise viewing of our own inner activity.

An alert observation of our own soul processes makes clear the *fact* that every judgment and also every choice within a greater whole take place through thinking. The problem is that we 'only' have thinking as our instrument with which to make choices and judgments, whether we direct this thinking to everything else or to thinking itself.

With this, we are already entering the area in which we cognize what thinking is. The difficulty that we want to get to know thinking *without* using abstract judgments, will pursue us continuously during our researches; however, becoming conscious of this difficulty can set us on the right track in our search for the nature of thinking.

The starting point of our research is to identify the situation or location of thinking within everything else, without saying anything about the value of thinking or about the value of everything else. We pass no judgment, we describe the situation of thinking amongst everything else as impartially as possible, in order to be able to ask the first question as plainly as possible and to answer it.

To this end, I shall place myself once more at the point of transition between not-thinking and the onset of thinking. I notice immediately that my associations and my normal life of thoughts and imaginings want to fill up this emptiness of non-thinking. They force themselves upon me and disturb my feeling for freedom in the choice between not-thinking and thinking. Thus this realm of thought which forces itself upon me is not actually *free* thinking. It inflicts itself upon my not-thinking without the engagement of my own will. We assume that we succeed in sending this realm of thought away from our thinking void. We are free again in making the choice between not-thinking and thinking. If I decide fully consciously now to commence thinking, I become aware that I need a *content* to be able to think. But I do not know at all what thinking should do with this content: where do I get this content from, and how should I then relate to it? Should I describe it and comprehend it? Because I have no idea yet as to the value of my thinking and that precisely this is the object of my research, I cannot start thinking. I cannot focus my thinking on a content which I take from everything else, because the relation between thinking and content is not yet clear. For that reason I can do no other than choose thinking itself as the first content of my thinking.

Consequently, I return once more to the onset of thinking: *how* could I ever get to know my thinking if I did not first set it going; and how could I set it going if I did not first give it a content? Therefore, I decide to think a random content. This content in itself has no meaning whatever. It only has meaning insofar as it makes possible the commencement of thinking. We can best fulfil our task when we choose a content which consists of a simple concept, in order that the *content* of thinking will not predominate, in which case our attention would be distracted from the process of thinking itself to the content.

In modern philosophy one thinks that thinking *is* the content, or that the content is thinking. That thinking is an independent *activity*, independent of the content, is no longer experienced. It is not to prove theoretically that it is so; we want to encourage the reader to a consideration of his own thinking, in order to be able to determine by himself what the meaning of thinking is. Thus it is about the observation of thinking as activity; to awake this activity we need a content, but the content has only a purpose for the activating, not for itself.

So I decide to think a simple concept: I think the concept of the circle. A circle is the mathematical area delineated by points in a plane, all of which are equidistant from the middle of the area. Naturally, it is not a matter of merely reciting this geometrical definition, but of using the words to make the concept concrete through active imaginative thinking. Whoever looks at himself conscientiously after this thinking activity and observes what he has inwardly done during this thinking process, will notice that he has to bestir himself to be able to truly think this concept without falling back on the imagination of a particular circle. We cut ourselves loose from this particular circle, with a particular radius and form the pure abstract concept which contains all possible circles. This concept is abstract because we have detached it from a particular imagination; nevertheless, we cannot form it without using elements from life (mental images): we can understand the concept 'distance', for example, because we have had experiences of variable distances in our life which have taught us in life what 'distance' means. Through these experiences the concept has acquired content.

At this point in our argumentation it is really essential that the reader tests for himself these statements about thinking and does not simply accept or reject them as theses. The difficulty with this is that he must not fall back on his already existing opinions about this, but must learn to proceed from a strictly objective, research perspective. Pure self-knowledge must be practised. He will observe that forming the common concept of the circle, without seeing a particular circle inwardly, requires the capacity to detach himself from his imaginative life. In addition, he will observe that he cannot think this common abstract concept without making use of mental representations which we have acquired from our experiences in life. We find an interweaving of concept and percept which we must raise into consciousness if we wish to cognise thinking.

Much more strongly than in thinking mathematical concepts we find this interweaving of concept and percept when we focus on a concept that can *exclusively* be known through a sense organ. As an example of this formation of concepts, I shall select the description of *white* by J.W. von Goethe[5].

1.
"There seems nothing easier than to make clear to oneself what one understands by 'white' and to discuss it with others; and yet it is extraordinarily difficult, for reasons which can only be explicated step by step and finally clarified at the end of this discourse. May I request impartial attention be given to the method and process of my lecture.

2.
First we take a transparent, colourless body such as water and we note (from refraction) that through a certain mass of water, we clearly perceive the conditions of its form and colour, so that a body at its highest degree of transparency is for the eye no longer a body and can only be discovered through feeling.

3.
The purest water may in its smallest parts pass over into solidity and impenetrability and we will then have snow, the piles of which represent for us the purest surfaces which now give us a perfect and indestructible concept

of whiteness. When their crystallisation water withdraws from them, transparent crystals transform themselves in the same way, e.g. as with Glauber's miracle salt, into a brilliant white powder.

4.

These bodies return again under changed circumstances from the white impenetrable condition into the state of colourless transparency. We draw the white bodies from the transparent colourless ones; we draw them back to transparency, and this direct relationship, this return to the transparent state is worth all our attention.

5.

Besides these white bodies, which we can see emerge from transparency and return to it again, there are many others which can be transformed into the white state, sometimes through water, light and air, which operation we call bleaching, whereby all parts which we can call more or less coloured are drawn out and separated from them, and sometimes through powerfully active agents, which effect a similar operation.

6.

All these actions, of which the chemist can give a more detailed account, produce an effect which impresses upon us together with the concept of white also the concepts of unalloyed purity and simplicity, so that in the realm of morality we have associated the concept of white with those of simplicity, innocence and purity.

7.

White has the greatest sensitivity for light, a characteristic that has been sufficiently remarked upon by researchers of nature and has been determined and expressed in various ways. It will suffice for us here to mention that a white surface (amongst which we may understand to approximate most closely to freshly fallen snow) amongst all other surfaces, whether grey, black or coloured, when placed next to them under the same light, is the brightest, to such an extent that its impress remains visible to the eye even in the darkest night or disappears last of all.

8.

White has a similar sensitivity to the touch of all bodies from which the colour is running, whether black, grey or otherwise coloured; the slightest line, the least spot will be noticeable on the white. Everything that is not white shows itself instantly on what is white, and it therefore remains the testing stone for all other colours and shades.

Try to form a clear concept of white *without* allowing in the thought of a white that you have ever observed. Through practice, one can succeed in abstracting the concept of white from the observation or imagination: that is to say, to think white without seeing white. But if you were blind from birth, would you ever be able to *understand* white? One would have to resort to metaphors and symbols in order to think the quality of 'white'.

Through this passage of Goethe I wanted to show how powerfully understanding and observation are interwoven in one's thinking.

In the foregoing we tried to think without mingling in imaginations derived from observation. Now we will try – in our investigation of the situation of thinking amongst the other things in life – to observe other things *without the activation of thinking* i.e. we are striving here for a perception without thoughts. I therefore step back again into the void of the not-thinking and then open my senses to everything beyond my thinking, to 'everything else'. I use my senses, but I do *not* think.

What reveals itself to me then is *pure perceptual content*, which is *nowhere* penetrated by thought. I perceive a chaos of impressions which lacks any inner connection at all. There is no here or there, no today or tomorrow, I do not know *what* I am seeing or tasting, there is no more or less, no differentiating qualities, no actions, no relations etc. In this chaos of impressions my inner perceptions, i.e. my thoughts, feelings and wishes are also present, but I cannot differentiate between internal and external, between me and the other, between I and the world, material and spiritual, etc.

It is not at all easy to take this step inward; there is an energetic education from the inner observation needed. Our thinking is not so powerfully under our control that we can turn it on and off at will. Nevertheless, anyone who wants to can form a lively imagination of this state of observation and not-thinking. This imagination then forms the transition to a true *establishing of the experience*. We need this lively experience if we want to lay the foundations of a philosophy which is not founded on mental abstractions, but which is rooted in the truth. When we stand amongst everything else *without* thinking, we experience a chaos of sense impressions. As soon as we start to make differentiations within this chaos, we engage our thinking, and it is of the greatest importance to become aware of that. In normal life observation is always permeated by thinking. Adults can no longer simply perceive without thoughts. That this is so, we can only experience when we can switch off thinking freely. We can, however, *understand* it beforehand if we imagine it in a lively way. This thinking, which goes on during perception and which precedes every science, differentiates sense impressions, systematises and categorises them. It does the same for psychic impressions. It is not yet a judging or a concluding, it is purely an ascertainment of the phenomena. It brings order into perceptions, it categorizes them.

The systematic grouping of the categories of thinking themselves, as they are used by us during thinking perception stems from   Aristotle. We quote from chapter 4 of this work of Aristotle, the Categories[6]:

"Every word spoken without combination signifies either substance, or quantity, or quality, or relation, or place, or time, or position, or state, or action, or passion. To give an approximate idea, examples of substance are 'man' or 'the horse', of quantity, such terms as 'two cubits long' or 'three cubits long', of quality, such attributes as 'white', 'grammatical'. 'Double', 'half', 'greater', fall under the category of relation; 'in the market place', 'in the Lyceum', under that of place; 'yesterday', 'last year', under that of time. 'Lying', 'sitting' indicate position, 'shoed', 'armed' indicate a state, it is the category of having; 'to cut', 'to burn', action; 'to be cut', 'to be burned', passion.

No one of these terms, in and by itself, amounts to an affirmation or a negation; it is by the combination of these terms that positive or negative statements arise. For every assertion or negation, it seems, must be either true or false, whereas only words which are not in combination, such as 'man', 'white', 'runs', 'wins', cannot be true or false."

At this point it is possible that doubt will take the upper hand and asks: 'Who says that this is a correct comprehensive description of thinking? Who says me that Aristotle is not mistaken here?'

Now comes the point where we can engage fully that which we have prepared as the wonder-filled, questioning, yet exact philosophical attitude, because here, doubt appears to thinking itself. We experience insecurity about the truth when we seek to know in relation to everything else in the world, so why, when it comes to thinking, should we now suddenly presume that the Aristotelian Categories are *true* and *comprehensive*?

That we experience insecurity in knowing everything in the world is caused by the fact that we do not participate in the creation of the world, or at least, we participate in it only slightly. A feeling that arises within me does not appear because I create that feeling consciously, but because it is activated by something inside or outside of me. I am in this

69

case 'direct object'; it is happening *to* me.

With regard to my actions, the case is not different. Many of my actions are necessities because they stem from impulses that *I* have not created but which come from the world or from within my person. So, paradoxically, it may seem that even in my actions, I am a passive object though *I* am the one carrying out the action; I am the actor. I see my actions as *my* work, but I do not *fully* take part in realizing the result. Also, the transmission of my intentions into my limbs does not occur in full consciousness: there is a deep gap between my conscious plans and the eventual execution of my actions.

With regard to 'the world outside me', I have a still greater insecurity in knowing. The beautiful chestnut tree in my garden is not *my* creation. Even if I have planted the chestnut myself from which the tree has grown, if I have followed every stage of sprouting, rooting, and growing, there still is a gap between my observations of the growth of the little tree and the *real* creative powers which make the little tree become a mature tree. That is why I am not 'sure' if these developments are exclusively physical and chemical processes, or if it is a matter of supersensible, supra-physical, supra-chemical creative forces. I am not the chestnut tree myself; I do not bring about this growth myself. Consequently, there is a naïve security in my understanding with regard to the being of the tree. It is actually there for me; I can touch it with my own hands, see it with my eyes and so on.

However, I have lost all security with regard to the *origin* of the tree, and if my naivety finally transforms itself into a critical attitude in cognition, I even start to doubt the actual being of the tree. 'Is it even there? Or is it only my imagination? Or is its reality different from mine and will I never be able to get through to *its* reality?' (the Kantian 'thing-in-itself'). In the same way, I lose my security with regard to my actions, my feelings and their origins.

Everything else in life (beyond my thinking) seems to be a reality, as it were, a tangible reality, but *I* am not totally present in its emergence. I cannot fully penetrate it with concepts. Part of it eludes my powers of perception.

As a naïvely observing person I have – because of this 'tangibility' – still a certainty about the reality nature of everything else in life, but not, however, about the how it comes into being. As a critically thinking person, I also lose this certainty with regard to the reality nature of everything else in life; I have no certainty in knowing left at all.

That we experience insecurity in our efforts to understand thinking has its roots in the fact that the 'matter' of thinking is elusive at first, that it is immaterial. We cannot grasp it with our hands or see it with our eyes. It can even withdraw itself from our observation for a lifetime if we do not *ourselves* make it the subject of research. Only this fact makes it understandable that in our time, in which we live so strongly with our observation directed to the outside world, thinking is experienced as a semblance, as an untouchable semblance. And how can that which originates in a semblance, namely knowledge, ever be more than an illusion, again mere appearance?

As a naïve human being I had certainty with regard to the

71

existence of a tangible reality. I lost this certainty when I started asking myself questions about knowing. Even the naïve human being has no certainty about the meaning of thinking. Is it possible for us as critical thinkers to develop this certainty out of precisely this critical standpoint?

Now comes the point where we engage the forces at our disposal and move ourselves into the transition from not-thinking to thinking. When we are able to enter into this transition energetically, we sense through thinking itself, through *thinking-as-seeing*, and understanding without the help of concepts, that if I want to think, then *I,* and no-one else, am the one who has to set thinking in train. Here is absolute freedom: I can start thinking or even not start. There is no other single cause for this engagement in thinking than my own will to engage in it. That this fact remains unnoticed in daily life is because the transition from not-thinking to thinking always escapes our attention because it is never simply present by itself. To be able to research this transition we have to bring it about ourselves and it requires much effort to do this, because we have continually to differentiate our thought associations, which are not penetrated by our will, from our true, free thinking. But for everyone who wants to do this, there is the possibility of finding this point, the wellspring of free thinking. Then he will find him*self as thinker*.

And one realises: here I have found the point in the world where I myself am the creator. It is no more than a point, but it is the point where I am conscious for the first time that: here I have found my actual human being. I recognise my very own thinking capacity, and from this moment on, nothing is the same as before.

Before I had found this point, I lived in insecurity about the world and about myself and the relation between them both. *At* this point I find myself as a free creating being. And precisely because I am the creator myself, there is no single inexplicable point in regard to what I create. After it has been thought, I do not have to think it over and understand it again as if it were something that had been created beyond my will and my being. That is the case with everything else, but not with thinking. No, while thinking is going on, it is wanted and known at the same time. What I think is not a creation which has to be understood subsequent to my creating it; rather, *it is not at all possible for me to think something that I do not already understand while thinking.*

I can certainly observe something that I do not understand; I can also repeat something that I do not understand; I can speak of something that I do not understand. Even a thought association which I do not understand can occur to me. But I can never *think* something myself that I have not already understood.

To realize this means to overcome forever the phenomenon of doubt. I am, as thinker, not only fully present in creating, but I also know exactly what I create *and* I know that this creation, my thinking, moves in accordance with *a lawfulness that is fully comprehended by me.* The seemingly unbridgeable gap between creation and concept, between world and I, between object and subject, *is here reliably bridged.*

The contradiction between Platonist and Aristotelian thinking is also resolved here: when we find our thinking as a reality that is at the same time both *subjective – I* construct it, and *objective* – it conforms to a lawfulness that lies outside of myself – then we become 'universal-realists'. We experience an objective general being – thinking – as a being which is different from everything else, because we produce it subjectively, while at the same time it obeys a general lawfulness.

Plato experienced universals as 'ante res': there is not only the reality of everything else, there is a second region of being, the world of Ideas, which precedes the creation of everything else. First, there was the Idea and out of this Idea was created the whole world of 'everything else'.

We experience this world of Ideas in our thinking as 'I myself, existent *before* the onset of thinking', thus as 'Ego, ante rem'.

By contrast, Aristotle found the *universalia in rebus* (universals in things): there is indeed a world of Ideas; however, it is not independent of and beyond everything else but is incorporated within the things of our world. We experience *ourselves* creating within thinking. We find our creative I incorporated in thinking. The I, my creative I, was there before I started thinking. It was there in not-thinking, it even brought the not-thinking about. The I was there as *universale ante rem*. Subsequently, the

74

I bestirs itself to work. Thinking, as a revelation of the universals of everything else, becomes a creation of the I. The I is *universalis in re*. It metamorphoses itself in full consciousness in the universals. During this process the self *and* its metamorphoses in the universals are understood in full consciousness, because thinking and understanding are indissolubly interconnected here. The I is *universalis post rem*. The I is the creator of thinking; thinking is itself 'I'. The Categories (of Aristotle) are the I, they are the letters with which the human being may write his own name *and* at the same time they are the name of the world. They are the letters of the 'cosmic word', the letters of the Logos. They are the letters of logic.

The self can release itself from its own creating activity and look upon what it has created. This observation is then at the same time an observation *and* a thinking understanding.

The human being who has *actually* found this point – thus not only as an imagination but really as a deed – brings to light that which normally lights up everything else but which always remains in the dark itself. When the light of thinking shines upon itself, it is released from the dark, where it is always experienced as surface appearance, and becomes a new observable substance, which is immaterial, and thus intangible to the bodily senses, but very 'tangible' to the sense of thought, the sense which *is* the self.

Thinking as metamorphosis of the I becomes Being.

Thinking differs from everything else because it is cognised through and through, for *I myself am it,* and it arises when I create myself. That is why there is *no* point of doubt anymore, because everything that is brought into being stands fully in the light of myself as thinker. That is why thinking about thinking is in no way comparable to thinking about everything else in life.

Nevertheless, it is also a fact that thinking is judged according to a transcendental criterion, as Edmund Husserl demands of a true theory of knowledge. The I must transcend itself to a point 'beyond' thinking – as we have done and described – to a point from which it illuminates thinking itself. The thinking by which thinking is judged is no other thinking than the thinking by which everything else in life is judged. The I only has to learn to transcend itself: it must learn to observe and contemplate its own activity, in which it always lives. Because the I is at the same time both creator *and* observer, this observing-contemplating is an activity through which the I causes itself to appear as a being. Here we come upon the two categories which are lacking in the Aristotelian doctrine of the Categories, namely, the two categories – *being and appearance* – which must be added to the ten Aristotelian Categories. The ten categories provide the letters of the alphabet with which everything else in the world is described, understood, and thought over. The *two new categories,* being and appearance, introduced by Hegel, provide the two categories with which we can comprehend thinking, can comprehend the I. These two categories are the ultimate transcendent criterion: the being of the I transcends and appears to himself in thinking about thinking.

At the end of this presentation of the first question and its answer we must focus on the similarity and difference between the observation of seeing our thinking and the observation of *thinking* about thinking which has been described above.

When I direct my perceptive capacity onto the *content* of my own consciousness, I am able - through practice – to become aware of my observation of the processes of consciousness themselves, of myself as observer of thinking. I notice then that this observation is always *active*, that *I* myself am the observer, but that this activity always escapes my observation unless I turn inwards spiritually and focus on the observation of consciousness itself. Here the activity consists of *devoted attention*. When, on the other hand, I move over from a state of not-thinking to thinking, my activity becomes a will to think. After I created it, I can perceive it. My activity becomes attention to *my* creation. This perceptive attention is at the same time *thinking* attention. What is perceived no longer needs to be understood, because *I have already thought it.*

I discover that thinking of thinking and observation of consciousness are both active processes, which are produced by the same power of my I. We experience this power, simultaneously, as pure thinking power, pure will-power, and pure power of perception.

To discover this point in consciousness is the alpha and omega of philosophy: it is both the starting point and the completion. Here, where doubt is overcome, we find the access point to a *knowledge of everything else in life.*

77

In the next chapter we will compare the first question and its answer, which we have now found, to the starting points of philosophical enquiry as presented by four great personalities, namely, G.W.F. Hegel, M. Heidegger, J. Krishnamurti and R. Steiner.

GEORG FRIEDRICH WILHELM HEGEL

There is evidence a-plenty in the works of Georg Friedrich Wilhelm Hegel that he himself found the point that we have described above. In order to understand Hegel, it is necessary to understand this point. In his works 'The Phenomenology of Spirit' and his 'Science of Logic' he only outlined this point, but nevertheless it constitutes the beginning and end of his thought. Even when one is not able fully to to take the step that Hegel takes in his thinking, one encounters a mighty content in his work that can enrich one's thinking. The essential significance of Hegel's work is not primarily to be found in its content, but in its process. By means of the content Hegel shows us, how very *differently* we must learn to think if we want to be able to judge thinking according to a 'transcendental criterion'.

In this book I seek to make just this *step* visible, which among others Hegel has taken in thinking. Only when we have taken this step in thought can we make real sense of Hegel's difficult sentences. In his own words:
'Unsere Kenntniss soll Erkenntniss werden. Wer mich kennt, wird mich hier erkennen.'[7] ("Our knowledge must become understanding. Whoever knows me will here understand me.")

On the one hand, in our time, because of the weakness in people's thinking which originates from instruction based on looking at things, in the cinema, on television etc., we have even more problems than the contemporaries of Hegel to understand his thinking; on the other hand, our need, our longing for a broadening of thinking is greater than ever before.

From The Science of Logic, part 1, page 34[8]:

"Before these dead bones of logic can be quickened by spirit, and so become possessed of a substantial, significant content, its method must be that which alone can enable it to be pure science. In the present state of logic one can scarcely recognise even a trace of scientific method. It has roughly the form of an empirical science. The empirical sciences have found for their own appropriate purposes their own peculiar method, such as it is, of defining and classifying their material. Pure mathematics, too, has its method which is appropriate for its abstract objects and for the quantitative form in which alone it considers them. I have said what is essential in the preface to the *Phenomenology of Spirit* about this method and, in general, the subordinate form of scientific method which can be employed in mathematics; but it will also be considered in more detail in the logic itself. Spinoza, Wolff and others have let themselves be misled in applying it also to philosophy and in making the external course followed by Notion-less quantity, the course of the Notion, a procedure which is absolutely contradictory.
Hitherto philosophy had not found its method; it regarded with envy the systematic structure of mathematics, and, as we have said, borrowed it or had recourse to the method

of sciences which are only amalgams of given material, empirical propositions and thoughts — or even resorted to crude rejection of all method.

However, the exposition of what alone can be the true method of philosophical science falls within the treatment of logic itself; *for the method is the consciousness of the form of the inner self-movement of the content of logic.*

In the *Phenomenology of Spirit* I have expounded an example of this method in application to a more concrete object, namely to consciousness. Here we are dealing with forms of consciousness each of which in realising itself at the same time resolves itself, has for its result its own negation — and so passes into a higher form. All that is necessary to achieve scientific progress — and it is essential to strive to gain this quite *simple* insight — is the recognition of the logical principle that the negative is just as much positive, or that what is self-contradictory does not resolve itself into a nullity, into abstract nothingness, but essentially only into the negation of its *particular* content, in other words, that such a negation is not all and every negation but the negation of a specific subject matter which resolves itself, and consequently is a specific negation, and therefore the result essentially contains that from which it results; which strictly speaking is a tautology, for otherwise it would be an immediacy, not a result. Because the result, the negation, is a *specific* negation, it has *content*. It is a fresh Notion but higher and richer than its predecessor; for it is richer by the negation or opposite of the latter, therefore contains it, but also something more, and is the unity of itself and its

81

opposite. It is in this way that the system of Notions as such has to be formed — and has to complete itself in a purely continuous course in which nothing extraneous is introduced.

I could not pretend that the method which I follow in this system of logic — or rather which this system in its own self follows — is not capable of greater completeness, of much elaboration in detail; but at the same time I know that it is the only true method. *This is self-evident simply from the fact that it is not something distinct from its object and content*; for it is the inwardness of the content, the dialectic which it possesses within itself, which is the mainspring of its advance. It is clear that no expositions can be accepted as scientifically valid which do not pursue the course of this method and do not conform to its simple rhythm, *for this is the course of the subject matter itself.*"

A lack of willpower in thinking makes it hard to follow this pure conceptual language and to understand not only its content but also its deeper meaning. When we have finally understood these sentences, we have still not yet got to the bottom of the meaning, for we shall only find this when we make what we have understood *into inner experience*. The truth in the sentence reveals itself by doing this. By referring to a number of sentences from the above–quoted passage, I shall make an effort to show that *Hegel* actually had his own inner experience of the point in thinking which we found in 'Philosophia', the previous chapter of this book.

'*However, the exposition of what alone can be the true method of philosophical science falls within the treatment of logic itself; for the method is the consciousness of the form of the inner self-movement of the content of logic.'*

Whoever wants to make this sentence an inner experience, can not restrict himself to the mere understanding of it. Here, we have to raise ourselves from our own inner, comfortable seats. One must raise oneself inwardly through an activation of the imaginative life in order to learn *to experience* these concepts. For Hegel it *is* experience, and from that experience he can in relatively few words state what he has realized. We have to form many imaginative pictures from these few words in order to realise this experience within ourselves.

One could object that Hegel employs the *premise* that the concepts are inwardly mobile and that the content of logic is the result of this inner mobility. This, objection can, however, only be made by one who approaches Hegel's texts only with *abstract,* non-experiential thinking. When one thinks abstractly and consequently does not *experience* anything, then the text is separated from the reader; it becomes something outside the reader. The sentences become something foreign to the reader, who then feels entitled to judge them with his own thinking as if they were something that had nothing to do with him. He overlooks the fact that the issue here is about *thinking in general,* about logical thinking, thus also about *his* logical thinking. That he continually employs this logical thinking in himself; the region that is to be researched therefore lives inside the reader, and is thus to be tested in self-knowledge.

When, for example, we read an account of a journey

through India, we can develop a lively imagination of the country described, but it will only become our own experience when we visit the country ourselves.

Hegel's work is a description of a trip in logical thinking that he himself had taken. For the reader, it will only become his own inner experience when, with Hegel as his guide, he makes this journey himself. For this we need a right vehicle. We have to practice perception of our own consciousness. This capacity is hidden in every human being, just as the capacities to learn to walk, speak and think are hidden in every new-born baby. While this learning to walk, speak and think unfolds naturally in infancy, the human being can only consciously teach *himself* to observe the activity of his own consciousness. We have to awaken this capacity if we do not wish to fall from mere slumber into deep sleep.

As we think through the quotation from Hegel *ourselves* in our active thinking, and, as it were, recreate it ourselves, we ourselves experience that logical thinking is the only true method of philosophical science, and that philosophy is only possible when we seek the method of logical thinking, the lawfulness of human thinking. When one thinks logically, when one practices logical thinking, not only trying to understand, but also trying to perceive one's own activity of logical thinking, one *sees* with one's inner eye, which is developed through this trying to perceive, how logical concepts – as the content of consciousness – themselves move, link up with each other, and one finds the form of the inner mobility of the content. Becoming aware of this – the fruit of self-perception – is the answer to the first question, a question without which no beginning is possible in philosophy, for this becoming aware is the very method of philosophical science. This experience makes possible a subsequent experience, which we can have in thinking through the following quotation from Hegel's "Science of Logic":

"*Logic is pure knowledge*, that is, pure knowing in the entire range of its development. But the result of this Idea is a certainty which has become truth, a certainty which, on the one hand, no longer confronts an object but has internalised it, knows it as part of its own self — and, on the other hand, has given up the cognising of itself as something confronting the object, of which it is only the annihilation, has relinquished this subjectivity and is at one with its relinquishing. So that the beginning of knowledge may remain immanent in this definition of pure knowing, there is nothing more to do than to consider what is there before us, or rather - by putting aside all reflections, all opinions which one otherwise has - merely to take it in.

Pure knowing, concentrated in this unity, has done away with all notion of other and of mediation; it is without any differentiation and as such, thereby ceases to be knowing; what is present is only simple immediacy. Simple immediacy is itself an expression of reflection and involves differentiation from what is mediated. The true expression of this simple immediacy, therefore, is *pure being*. Just as pure knowing should be called knowing as such, quite abstract, so too pure being should be called nothing other than *being* itself: being, and nothing else, without any further specification and content."

Logic is pure knowledge, knowing in its purest form, because logic is the doctrine of the very art of knowing, and this art of knowing is at the basis of all sciences. Pure knowing is the consciousness of *how* the concepts themselves move; it is therefore logic. And because this reveals itself directly in self-perception, thus without reflection, this pure knowing is 'certainty which has become truth'. Certainty, because it is not necessary, in order to understand it, to think over again this pure knowing perceiving it as a pure movement of thought. No, this movement of thinking speaks itself out while thinking, and is at the same time thought out and understood. It is truth because at the moment that one experiences this, one *has the pure knowing* that here the I and the world, which are divided from each other in every other situation in life, and give rise to doubt precisely through this division, are one. In this point one is sure of the truth.

However, in his *Science of Logic* Hegel states that pure knowing is the starting point for logic. This is the first step in his philosophy. He describes it as 'simple immediacy' (*einfache Unmittelbarkeit*), This starting point corresponds to what I have called the condition of 'not knowing', the thought-void or 'pre-philosophical' state in which I find myself as a questioning human being, without a concrete content in my consciousness being present, without a concrete question. I *am* indeed, but I am inwardly silent, motionless. This motionless silence is Hegel's "pure being, being and nothing else, without any further specification and content" (*reines Sein, Sein, sonst nichts, ohne alle weitere Bestimmung und Erfüllung*)

Hegel is fully aware that the positing of this state as pure being (*reines Sein*), is based on a reflection, on a definition reached through thinking. Through this, in the moment of this reflection, *I* step forward out of pure being. This moment, this point, which is of the greatest importance at the beginning of philosophy here remains unclear. Is this reflection and the conclusion from it obvious so that it can not be doubted? If so, why? Because it still is *my* reflection! I myself have stepped forward out of pure being, I have observed what I experienced there and determined this. *I have become active.*

According to Hegel, the logic would think itself. I would then be guided from pure being to the next concept by the power lying in the concept 'pure being' itself. Either I have to accept this – if I have understood it – from Hegel, or I will have to be able to make it my own experience. But if I choose the latter option, if I place myself in the state of pure being, or at the point of not-thinking, I will *not* be able to experience it myself. The mobility of the logical concepts themselves will not become an experience in my thinking just like that.

It *is* possible to remain in this condition of not-thinking, to abstain from all reflection and not to go on to the next concept. *I* am stronger than the power which lives in the concept 'pure being'. Indeed, *I am myself the force which has formed the concept 'pure being'*. I am not subject to the movement of concepts: I myself produce this movement. I am the driving force in the movement of concepts. When engaged in the act of thinking, it is I who has to *want* to proceed.

87

It is precisely the discovery that I am completely responsible for the creation of my thoughts and that I know my creation through and through, that makes me sure about the truth; it brings me to 'the certainty that has become truth'. I find here the full development of my I in the truth: I do not think randomly, but I live in the lawfulness of thinking, which is my own lawfulness. I think the truth and know that it is truth. I experience my source in the truth and that my pure I wants nothing else as to metamorphose itself in true concepts.

In philosophy the first question that must be asked is the question about thinking itself. If we ask this question rightly, we find the right answer in the asking. And this answer makes clear the relation between the I and thinking. *I* set thinking in train, I move it and transform *myself* into the concepts. The subjective self becomes objective in the concepts. When this answer becomes experience, doubt is overcome.

MARTIN HEIDEGGER

For Martin Heidegger the first question lies in a totally different area. As a twentieth century thinker, he maintains a greater distance between himself as thinker, and that which he thinks about. Because of this distance, and because of the fact that Hegel's philosophy lacks one thing, as described above, namely, it lacks the question and the answer as to the origin of the movement of logical concepts, Heidegger can not understand Hegel and therefore comes to the statement[9]:

"And when Hegel determines Being to be 'the indetermined immediate' and places this determination at the basis of all his further categorical explications of his 'Logic', he thus holds to the same perspective as the ontology of the ancients, except that he loses sight of the problem that Aristotle already posited about the problem of the unity of Being in relation to the plurality of the Categories."

Apparently, Heidegger has not had the *experience* of the 'indetermined immediate' as pure being, and this remains for him an abstraction that can be doubted. Therefore, he does not see, because of the lack of this step from the abstract into the absolute concrete, that the experience of pure being is achieved and that this pure being as pure knowing *is* just this 'unity of being', from which the 'plurality of the Categories' can be developed, whereby also doubt will eventually be overcome in the sciences of everything else besides logic.

For Hegel, pure being as pure knowing is the origin of science and thus becomes direct certainty. Heidegger, by contrast, finds pure being when all certainty is taken from man, thus he finds it to be the most extreme consequence of doubt. That both may be correct, because they are talking about a different concept although the word 'being' is the same, may be obvious. Hegel finds a universal certainty in thinking being. Heidegger finds being when one experiences oneself in the naked impermanence of one's own existence.

For Heidegger, 'being' means the transitory, physical experience of existence, of the concrete experience of life. He cannot find the experience of being as a concrete being in thinking.

Heidegger *describes and thinks over* in a genial and comprehensive way the question of being, but remains in his thinking distant from his own being. He therefore does not find himself in the instrument of his cognising and thereby remains a spectator. Even his own human being is viewed from the outside. Heidegger:[10]

"'Being' can not be determined to the point where beingness is attributed to it. Being is definitively not to be derived from higher concepts nor is it to be represented through lower (ones)."

In other words, being can neither be defined deductively, nor inductively.

According to Heidegger, the first question is therefore the question about being, whereby questioning is itself a way of being and is carried out by a questioner who is at the same time a way of being.[11]

"This existent [Seiende], which we ourselves always are, and which amongst other things has the existent possibility of questioning, we term 'Dasein' (existence). A specific and clear formulation of a question as to the meaning of being demands a prior, appropriate explanation of an existent (Dasein) with regard to his being."

Here Heidegger realises that this may give rise to endless regression, a 'going round in circles'.

"In fact, however, in the formulation of a question referred to there is no circle at all. The existent can be determined in its being without the explicit concept of the meaning of being having to be already available. Were this not so, there could not until now have been any ontological knowledge, the factual existence of which will not be denied."

Heidegger makes clear his path here: he does not search for a starting point where doubt can be overcome so that the subsequent statements no longer need to be doubted; the human being, 'Dasein', as participant in being, steps forward by itself out of the whole, and indeed as the first participant, who must be determined because he is the questioner. With regard to the content, Heidegger comes to the same conclusion as Hegel, although he formulates it in a different way:

"The understanding of being is itself a determination of

the being of *Dasein*. Being itself (*das Sein*), to which *Dasein* can relate in this or that manner and to which it always somehow relates, we call *existence* (Existenz)."

The understanding of one's own being is called 'existential'. The connection of the structures which together form existence, Heidegger calls 'existentiality' (*Existentialität*). With this formulation he comes to the following statement:[13]

"Only when the philosophical research questioning itself is grasped existentially as an existential possibility of *Dasein* existent at any time is there the possibility of a development of the existentiality of existence and thereby the possibility of the beginning of an adequately based ontological problematic. However, the ontic precedence of the question of being is also made clear by this."

(Ontic = rooted in a specific form of being, in this case, in philosophical questioning. Or: understanding of one's own being through one's state of being of form of existence (*Dasein*). Ontological = an understanding of that part of the being which lies outside the *Dasein*.)

One could say that this very complicated mode of expression points to the distance from which thinking about the philosophical starting point commences. With regard to content, Heidegger here writes as *ideal* what Hegel formulates as *result*.

Hegel:[14] "In its true expression therefore this simple immediacy is pure being. Just as pure knowing has to mean nothing but knowing itself, totally abstract (this is Hegel's answer to Heidegger's *'ontic* question', or the existential understanding of the possibility of being of the always existing Dasein - author), similarly, pure being should not mean anything else but being itself; being, nothing else, without any further determination whatsoever.' (this is Hegel's answer to Heidegger's question about existence, his ontological question)."

Heidegger too regards human self-knowledge as the only starting point for philosophy. He concludes that this is the only possibility for a true philosophy. But he does not come any further than *understanding* this and proceeding with his line of thought from out of this concept. He does not succeed in coming to a true unification of this concept and the *activity of understanding itself as a real being*. If he had done this, he would have understood and experienced the truth and the validity of Hegel's statement – quoted above by Heidegger. He would then have been able to stand with Hegel, instead of distancing himself from him. When a philosopher becomes aware of the truth in *all* philosophical works, even though it may be a one-sided truth, then the cognizance and experiencing of any philosophical work whatsoever is an enrichment of the spirit. The way in which a philosopher approaches a question and the standpoint that he adopts we may not find pleasant. However, our ability to overcome this antipathy and to think along with and experience a philosophical content in an unprejudiced way, always helps us discover truth in thinking. We can thus learn to understand how another person finds the truth in a different way, from another point of view. Only then will it become clear to us how one comes to one-sided and half-truths. Heidegger could have understood Hegel. Here we try to understand both philosophers.

Working on the philosophy of a man like Heidegger, a man who during the Second World War sympathized with the National Socialists, is a very important example of such an absence of prejudice. As Heidegger thought, people *can* think, they think that way.

This thinking was not able to protect Heidegger from taking certain steps in his *life* with which one can not agree. There is only *one* way to investigate and understand the connection between Heidegger's thinking and his life, and that is to think along with his philosophy in a powerful but unprejudiced manner. That is actually then Heidegger's thinking, because one leaves one's own input out of consideration. Only in this way can the 'problem of Heidegger' be resolved. One could object that such an unprejudiced approach, whereby one's own point of view is given up, renders one uncritical and liable to lose oneself. This objection is only justified when one omits to *experience* what one in unprejudiced active thinking has understood. It is just this experience that brings us the reflection on the *nature* of thinking, and leads to an optimal critical clarity in which the I can maintain itself.

For Heidegger, the central point of philosophy is *being*, which stands 'above' the other Categories as such. The task of philosophy is then to come to a meaning of this being, of the 'Sinn des Seins'. But because this is, on the one hand, concretely, the closest and most obvious concept – it appears in almost *every* sentence – and on the other hand, it is, abstractly, the least understood concept, because it cannot be found by induction or by deduction, some other entry point for philosophy must be found, which reveals itself openly.

The philosophical research method Heidegger employs is *phenomenology*. This is based on an unprejudiced observation of phenomena, which speak for themselves, so that no arbitrary random element slips into the research.

In this way, according to Heidegger, the philosophical mode of enquiry reveals itself to be the human mode of being, which he calls 'Dasein'; this again is a mode of being in itself and the gateway to an explication of the meaning of being.

Here the powerlessness of the philosopher becomes clear. The philosopher searches for an explication of the centre of being, in which *everything* that is created has a share. Heidegger finds this centre within being itself, but experiences at the same time powerlessness in being unable to reach this phenomenon, which, as it were, underlies the entire Universe as an open secret, and which is at the same time the darkest concept we have.

Heidegger looks at this problem as from a distance; he sees being as an unclarified concept which lies at the root of all the other Categories and thinks that with the help of phenomenology from amongst the other Categories, he can illuminate the philosophical mode of enquiry as the mode of being of *Dasein* which forms the entry point for an illumination of the darkness of the concept of being. In this way, he thinks that he will be able to escape the problem of thinking. He sees phenomenology, as it were, as a learning to read reality.

What escapes from his attention here is that also in reading, in which process the human being surrenders unselfishly to 'what is written', *thinking* has to go on. One's own thinking cannot follow one's own arbitrary impulses, but has to comply with the letters, words, and sentences if we are to be able to understand what is written. We need thinking to *recognise* the letters and make them into words and subsequently combine the words in order to understand the sentences. Whoever wants to read without thinking, is staring at a page full of meaningless signs.

In this sense the human being stands before the phenomena of reality. He perceives them through his senses, but they would remain meaningless signs if he had not learned to read with the help of his thinking, which penetrates these signs with concepts. When one observes being as standing above the Categories, when one sees the philosophical mode of enquiry come forward as the mode of being of human existence (*Dasein*) - all this happens through thinking. It is impossible to highlight only *one* phenomenon from the totality of being and define it without using thinking. Even the mere highlighting of a phenomenon within the totality happens through thinking. This is why philosophy cannot begin otherwise than by a making aware, a becoming aware, of the place of thinking in the act of knowing. One thus has to apply phenomenology as a research method to thinking itself. In all the other Categories of being thinking must follow the phenomena; I must engage all my will to apply my thinking to the phenomena. Only in thinking itself do the phenomenon and thinking about the phenomenon coincide in full congruence.

If I can think thinking itself *free* of the senses, I create the phenomenon myself. I will not have to 'think about' it, because I know exactly how the phenomenon comes to life. In no other area of reality, of being, am I so fully present in the creative act as in thinking, wherein I do not only create the thought, but also *myself as thinker*. I could never claim that I create my own body but I *can* say: when my thinking is free of the senses, and when I observe this thinking consciously, then I know that *I* as thinker am the creator of my spiritual 'presence'. Only by creating itself like this over and over again does the soul become aware of itself and experiences itself fully as a spirit, as a being which can live in a completely sense-free region in which it no longer feels the emergence of a single memory of the life in the physical sense world, nor any content arising from that life.

In this spiritual 'presence of mind', in which the I coincides fully with its situation in the now, completely congruent with the experiencing of the moment, one finds thinking as *a pure experience of time* - thinking is *pure time*. The content of thinking streams to one out of the past. By contrast, one finds one's I, one's being as power that is not yet fulfilled, as *pure will*, streaming to one from the future. The interflow of these two streams - of being as pure will, and of thinking as pure thinking – gives us literally the *presence* of spirit, our pure living spirit in the now.

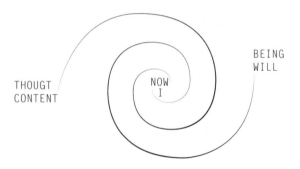

Fig. 2

With the aid of abstract phenomenology, Heidegger finds that time determines the meaning of being in human existence (*Dasein*). In other words, the meaning of human being is time. *Als der Sinn des Seins desjenigen Seienden, das wir Dasein nennen, wird die Zeitlichkeit aufgewiesen.* (The meaning of the being of that form of being which we call 'existence' is shown to be temporality).

In contrast to Heidegger's phenomenology, we put forward the concrete phenomenological method of thinking that is conscious of itself, a thinking which, after thorough practice, results in a conscious experience of *oneself as a thinker in the medium of time.*

KRISHNAMURTI

A totally different approach to the 'initial question' is the path taken by Krishnamurti, who has pointed out a way to change the quality of consciousness through which man can effect a change in world processes. Krishnamurti points to thinking as the cause of all conflict. He gives no further definition of what he means by thinking, but from his many lectures, it is clear that by 'thinking', he means, on the one hand, thinking with the intellect, abstract thinking, and on the other hand, associative thinking that is coloured by emotion. He acknowledges the value of abstract thinking for practical life, but rejects it completely as the bearer of higher ideals. The following thoughts about Krishnamurti's path are not meant as a critical attack; on the contrary, I have engaged intensively with the works of Krishnamurti and experienced them as a great support in a phase of my life when I was having to deal with much grief. In them one can find much that is exceptional, comforting and that has the effect of cleansing egoism. However, I found that they lack a step which we – as western people – must unavoidably take, and the lack of this step makes Krishnamurti's path not fully valid for western people. Krishnamurti says: (in 'Talks Saanen, 1974'):

"So from that arises the question: how does one listen to and look at one's consciousness? The speaker was born in a certain country where he absorbed all the prejudices, the irrationalities and the superstitions, the beliefs,

99

the class differences, as a Brahmin; there the young mind absorbed all this, the tradition, the rituals, the extraordinary orthodoxy and the tremendous discipline imposed by that group upon itself. And then he moves to the West, again he absorbs from all that is there; the content of his consciousness is what has been put into it, what he has learnt, what his thoughts are and the thought which recognises its own emotions and so on. That is the content and the consciousness of this person. Within that area he has all the problems, the political, religious, personal, communal, you follow? - all the problems are there. And not being able to solve them himself, he looks to books, to others, asking: ` Please tell me what to do, how to meditate, what shall I do about my personal relationship with my wife, or my girl-friend or whatever it is, between myself and my parents, should I believe in Jesus or in Buddha, or the new guru who comes along with a lot of nonsense?' - you follow? - searching for a new philosophy of life, a new philosophy of politics and so on, all within this area. And man has done this from time immemorial. There is no answer within that area. You may meditate for hours, sitting in a certain posture, breathing in a special way, but it is still within that area because you want something out of meditation. I do not know if you see all this?

So there is this content of unconsciousness, thought, dull, stupid, traditional, recognising all its emotions - otherwise they are not emotions - always it is thought, which is the response of memory, knowledge and experience, operating. Now, *can the mind look at it?* Can you look at

100

the operation of thought? Now, when you look, who is the observer who is looking at the content, is it different from the content? This is really a very important question to ask and to which to find an answer. Is the observer different from the content and therefore capable of changing, altering and going beyond the content? Or is it that the observer is the same as the content? First look: if the observer - the 'I' that looks, the 'me' that looks - is different from the observed then there is a division between the observer and the observed, therefore conflict - I must not do this, I should do that - I must get rid of my particular prejudice and adopt a new prejudice - get rid of my old gods and take on new gods. So when there is a division between the observer and the observed there must be conflict. That is a principle, that is a law. So, do I observe the content of my consciousness as if I were an outsider looking in, altering the pieces and moving the pieces to different places? Or am I the observer, the thinker, the experiencer, the same as that thought which is observed, experienced, seen?

If I look at the content of my consciousness as an outsider observing then there must be conflict between what is observed and the observer. So what happens when I hear this statement that when there is a division between the observer and the observed, there is conflict? There must be conflict; on that division and in that conflict we have lived, the 'me' and the 'not me', 'we' and 'they'. If 'I', the observer, am different from anger, I try to control it, suppress it, dominate it, overcome it and all the rest and here is conflict. But is the observer different at all; or is he essentially the same as the observed? If he is the same then there is no conflict, is there? The understanding of that is intelligence; then intelligence operates and not conflict.

It would be a thousand pities if you did not understand this simple thing. Man has lived 'in conflict' and he wants peace, through conflict, and there can never be peace through conflict - however much armament you may have, against another armament equally strong, there will never be peace.

Only when intelligence operates will there be peace - intelligence which comes when one understands that there is no division between the observer and the observed. This insight into that very fact, that very truth, brings this intelligence. Have you got it? *This is a very serious thing,* for then you will see you have no nationality - you may have a Passport but you have no nationality - you have no gods, there is no outside authority, nor inward authority. The only authority then is intelligence, not the cunning intelligence of thought, which is mere knowledge operating within a certain area - that is not intelligence."

In order to experience the value of the work of Krishnamurti, it is necessary now to reflect on the concept 'thinking'. Krishnamurti was, as he says himself, raised as a Brahmin in India and has a completely different content in his consciousness than Europeans have. No one would wish to object to that. But perhaps not only the *content of consciousness* is different, but also the relationship of the consciousness to one's own personality, perhaps the whole experience of the consciousness is different. In that case, it would be necessary to discover and cognise the differences between the Eastern and the Western consciousness, in order to understand what an Eastern human being can mean to a Western human being and vice versa. However, in order to accomplish this, one would have to have an objective method of perceiving one's own consciousness so that one can experience the quality of one's own consciousness and through an intensive living into the mode of consciousness of another, one can experience these qualities in their differences.

When a westerner simply follows what Krishnamurti says - that 'the observer and the observed coincide and all conflict thus ends', it will remain a *hypothesis* for the Westerner, which he can accept and try to realise in his life. But Krishnamurti does not want this. He asks us to *experience* this in reality and not to want to accept it on authority. The westerner's difficulty is that he absorbs everything in his consciousness *after having first abstracted it,* that is, after first making a mental representation of it. The westerner no longer experiences reality directly. That is both the tragedy and also the benefit of abstraction in thinking. *Every* impression which I receive, either from the outer world, or from the 'inner' world of feelings and will impulses, I make into a mental representation through my thinking. I can not take in any observation directly as reality; there is always mediation through mental representation. Let us enter the area of observation.

With my eyes I perceive light, darkness, and colours. What

103

happens to this observation in my sub-consciousness, I cannot follow at first, but I can follow what I experience in my consciousness. I see the red and I *know* that it is red. As a westerner, I have learned to emphasize the *knowledge* of red. As soon as I see something red, the mental representation 'red' adds itself to it, and subsequently, the concept 'red' or even the inner spoken word 'red'. This concept, this word, I experience as abstract, as cold, as empty, as a reflection of the reality of red. If I am accustomed to let the observations sink in deeper, I can observe how red brings me into a certain mood, how it touches my emotional life. But it does not go so far that, when I see something red, I become 'red' myself, as it were, either on the outside or on the inside. And in our fleeting daily existence the deeper experience of feelings also escapes our attention and I only have the mental representation and understanding of red. I *know* that I am looking at the colour 'red', but I experience this knowing as something that *I* put over against the reality of red; perhaps it has no meaning to the real 'red' at all?

This experience prompted Kant to call the true, actual red 'Ding an sich' (thing-in- itself). This thing-in-itself cannot be known; we can only know our imagination of it, and as soon as we become aware of it, painfully experience our separation from reality. We feel literally 'de-realized'.

This is the case both with inner and outer observations. When feelings arise within me, I do not know not with immediate certainty what they mean. I form mental imaginations of my feelings, so that I can understand them. Much of the work of psychologists and psychiatrists relates to learning to identify feelings and learning to deal with them. But it remains an *abstract* engagement with these feelings because we have to think *about* them after the fact. The results obtained remain questionable.

Everything I perceive as it occurs to me is wrapped in a mental representation. Through this I place myself *over against* what is perceived. That is the tragedy of the constitution of the westerner, because through this process everything remains questionable and subject to doubt; the process is thus conflict. Yet it is also the good fortune of the westerner, because he has the capability to make every perception into an object, separate it from himself, and thus find his *freedom* with regard to it. After all, a mere mental representation does not have the power to force us to anything whatsoever.

We therefore come to the conclusion that what Krishnamurti teaches is *true*, but that it does not have any further *validity* for the westerner. When one goes deeply into what Krishnamurti asks from us, when one 'puts it to the test' and therefore tries to make what is understood into deed and experience it, then one must admit to feelings of intense impotence. For, what is actually being asked from us?

First, we are called upon to look at our consciousness without creating new mental representations. For example, we look at our mental representations, perhaps also *how* we form them, but we may not do this by forming imaginations of the process itself, no, we must observe ourselves inwardly and *keep on* observing, *without forming mental representations, without reflection.* In the moment we pass from looking at something into forming a mental representation of it, we put ourselves over against it; the observer separates himself from the observed, and conflict is produced. In our time, the westerner's attention is so focused on the outer world that he sees the inner world fade immediately when he turns his view inside and therefore he stands before the void, with no content; and this void fills immediately with memories and imaginations from the outer world he wanted to turn away from. If we nevertheless want to say something about what we have experienced in our inner perception, nothing remains but the forming of abstract mental representations of it. This gives rise to modern 'scientific' psychology. The word 'scientific' is here between quotation marks, because the field to be researched, namely the psyche, withdraws from our observation like a dream every time we try to perceive. Thus nature gives us no possibility to perceive and hold on to our own consciousness directly, without reflection. We can accomplish this through practice, but it is not given naturally.

But this is not the only challenge Krishnamurti gives us. He does not only ask us to perceive our consciousness without reflecting on it, he asks us further not only to be conscious in this consciousness when perceiving it, but also to become aware of the observer himself and then to experience both in conjunction with each other, without effort, without practice, without striving. We must *see* how much we work inwardly, and at the same time we must *see* that we see this and realize that the one who sees and that what is seen are one.

If we already fall into impotence at the first step, the second and third we can at most understand, but not re-alise inwardly, not without practice, without striving. For that, we lack the natural talent. And because the westerner is not capable of doing this just like that, two dangers threaten him if he nevertheless wants to achieve it - without practice. Because he lacks the power to keep standing in the inner void and to observe the true powers that bear consciousness, he falls back, whether he notices it or not, into looking at memories of the outer world. With westerners, these are *always* abstractions of living reality. If he then tries to experience himself as observer and unite himself with the observed, he sticks himself internally to his abstractions, so to speak, he fixes himself to them. Instead of becoming one with the spiritual reality for which he is searching, (and which Krishnamurti, in my view, actually experienced) the westerner grows together around himself. He certainly finds himself, but not his spiritual reality, his spiritual self; he finds only the abstractions of his own personal life - his personal memories, predictions, wants, strivings.

There is a second danger – however paradoxical this may seem – in succeeding to answer Krishnamurti's challenge. Krishnamurti wants to bring love into western culture. He is an apostle of love and a fighter against thinking. He sees in thinking all the dangers of abstraction that thinking brings with it. And he sees this rightly. Because of the fact that we can think intellectually, we live with our consciousness outside the area of love, outside morality. The more intellect loosens itself from reality, the more readily man turns to logic to justify abstractly what is not right and good.

Nevertheless, the possibility for real human freedom lies precisely here. A man stands as I before the world, and has no notion any longer that his I *is* not only himself but also the world. He only has responsibility for himself. Only when he is able to find the source of morality in this I which has become separated from the world, is he himself a moral human being, a human being who is both free and *good*.

If the westerner responds to Krishnamurti's insistent call, he gives up his freedom too early, gives it up before he has realized the mission of abstraction, which is to discover freedom. If he gives up this mission too early, before he has understood what it means, he becomes one with the world, but loses himself, loses the possibility to make the choice between good and evil. He *must* be good and does not know any longer that he *wants* that. This is exactly what Krishnamurti calls freedom - freedom from the known, freedom from thinking. He shows the way back to the innocence of not knowing.

And he is right. For himself he is completely right. But the westerner must not go *back* to innocence, he must go *through* the guilt of knowing, becoming aware of his human capacity to have the courage to know what one knows and what one does not know. That is innocence renewed: the consciousness that one has become a human being in the now and, forever pushing at his boundaries, goes on becoming a human being into the future.

In order to realize this ideal one must become a philosopher. Full human consciousness lives in thinking, the human being lives fully consciously, even though it is abstract. In this thinking he will have to find the point with which true self-knowledge can connect so that he can survey his way ahead with certainty. He will have to learn to love this controversial thinking and in order to get to know it truly, learn to know it lovingly.

One has to have the *courage* to find the point of application *within* this life of abstract thinking where one can break through this life of abstract mental representations, break out of it. We will never find this point only by observing our mental representations. Neither will we find it in areas outside clear consciousness, because that would be to give up our wakeful, lucid awareness and our freedom.

If, by contrast, we find within our life of mental representations the one who is forming those representations, not only by observation of the representations, but by experiencing the point of the transition from not-thinking to thinking, and thus experience the profound union between the one who is forming the representations and the mental representations themselves; if we learn in such full, conscious awareness to make mental representations, that we ourselves are the representer, *then* we will find the point at which we know: I myself am creating these mental representations. And this knowing we achieve not through yet another mental representation, another mental image, but through experience of the direct willpower which produces the representation from itself. One then has the *first* true experience in mental representation, which is no longer merely any kind of mental positing, proposing or imagining, but a willed thinking, a powerful thinking that creates from the will, without intervening mental representations, without reflection, without conflict. Only from this point can we reach out to Krishnamurti and take up his call. We break through the reflecting surfaces of mental representations and find a depth beyond them from which truthful thinking wells up from the spring of our own I. Here, in this I where we no longer need mental representations, where we can simply *be* in full consciousness, there we are thinker and thought, perceiver and perceived, observer and observed at the same time. We can thus answer Krishnamurti's question in a way that is right for westerners. Here is the point where we can truly get through to the 'in-themselves' nature of things, where we ourselves are united with the 'thing-in-itself', and from where all the other 'things–in-themselves' are freed from being 'in-themselves'. This means the end of all conflict.

RUDOLF STEINER

The reader's capacity for unprejudiced judgment will again be called on strongly now, because reference will now be made to the work of a controversial thinker, who has received no place in the philosophical 'tradition' as a philosopher. We do not find his work on the literature lists of modern philosophers. Perhaps you already had certain preconceived ideas about Krishnamurti and it was hard for you to exclusively follow his pure line of thought, excluding pre-existing sympathies and antipathies. When we quote Rudolf Steiner, it will certainly be difficult for some readers who are not anthroposophists, to maintain an unprejudiced attitude. Who does not already have an opinion, whether well-founded or not, about Rudolf Steiner and anthroposophy? Anthroposophy is seen as a worldview, a philosophy of life, as faith, as dogmatic doctrine, as 'denominationalism', as fanaticism, as sectarianism, as heresy, as the highest spiritual legacy, as a path of development, and as philosophy; but anthroposophy is not acknowledged to be philosophy by professional philosophers.

Nevertheless I ask readers to turn off all these value judgments, to forget what they know about Rudolf Steiner and anthroposophy, *whether it is positive or negative,* and think along with the following quotation[22] in an unprejudiced way. The true philosopher *must* be able to be completely unprejudiced, or else he is no philosopher!

From Die Philosophie der Freiheit (The Philosophy of Freedom). (English edition 1939):[15]

"The peculiar nature of thought consists just in this, that the thinker forgets his thinking while actually engaged in it. It is not thinking which occupies his attention, but rather the object of thought which he observes.

The first point, then, to notice about thought is that it is the unobserved element in our ordinary mental life. The reason why we do not notice the thinking which goes on in our ordinary mental life is no other than this, that it is our own activity. Whatever I do not myself produce appears in my field of consciousness as an object; I contrast it with myself as something the existence of which is independent of me. It forces itself upon me. I must accept it as the presupposition of my thinking. As long as I think about the object, I am absorbed in it, my attention is turned on it. To be thus absorbed in the object is just to contemplate it by thought. I attend not to my activity, but to its object. In other words whilst I am thinking, I pay no heed to my thinking which is of my own making, but only to the object of my thinking which is not of my making.
I am, moreover, in exactly the same position when I adopt the exceptional point of view and think of my own thought-processes. I can never observe my present thought, I can only make my past experiences of thought-processes subsequently the objects of fresh thoughts. If I wanted to watch my present thought, I should have to split myself into two persons, one to think, the other

112

to observe this thinking. But this is impossible. I can only accomplish it in two separate acts. The observed thought-processes are never those in which I am actually engaged but others. Whether, for this purpose, I make observations on my own former thoughts, or follow the thought-processes of another person, or finally, as in the example of the motions of the billiard balls, assume an imaginary thought-process, is immaterial.

[...]

For every one, however, who has the ability to observe thought, and with good will every normal man has this ability, this observation is the most important he can make. For he observes something which he himself produces. He is not confronted by what is to begin with a strange object, but by his own activity. He knows how that which he observes has come to be. He perceives clearly its connections and relations. He gains a firm point from which he can, with well-founded hopes, seek an explanation of the other phenomena of the world.

[...]

When thought is made an object of observation, something which usually escapes our attention is added to the other observed contents of the world. But the usual manner of observation, such as is employed also for other objects, is in no way altered. We add to the number of objects of observation, but not to the number of methods. When we are observing other things, there enters among the world-processes — among which I now include observation — one process which is overlooked. There is present something different from every other kind of process, something which is not taken into account. But

113

when I make an object of my own thinking, there is no such neglected element present. For what lurks now in the background is just thought itself over again. The object of observation is qualitatively identical with the activity directed upon it. This is another characteristic feature of thought-processes. When we make them objects of observation, we are not compelled to do so with the help of something qualitatively different, but can remain within the realm of thought.

When I weave a tissue of thoughts round an independently given object, I transcend my observation, and the question then arises, what right have I to do this? Why do I not passively let the object impress itself on me? How is it possible for my thought to be relevantly related to the object? These are questions which every one must put to himself who reflects on his own thought-processes. But all these questions lapse when we think about thought itself. We then add nothing to our thought that is foreign to it, and therefore have no need to justify any such addition."

Rudolf Steiner bears witness to a step that he has taken in thinking, and which is not at all easy to understand, let alone follow. I am referring to his works 'A Theory of Knowledge Implicit in Goethe's World Conception', 'Truth and Science', and 'The Philosophy of Freedom'. These have remained mostly misunderstood books, in the sense that a practical handbook for inner transcendence such as 'The Philosophy of Freedom' actually is has been understood instead as a philosophical-theoretical work, with which one can either agree or not. It is, however, no theory, but a practical guide on that road to inner transcendence; but the value of the work is not recognised, and it is put aside.

Furthermore, the path which Rudolf Steiner went on subsequently to make clear as the path to higher insight – a path that he had taken and which had given him those insights into higher worlds – made it impossible for many people who see themselves as scientists, or as practical human beings, or as belonging to a certain community of faith, to maintain the unprejudiced attitude of mind which is necessary if one wants to be able to value these works rightfully and experience their effect. They are therefore only accepted by people who have familiarised themselves with Anthroposophy and have not received the attention and appreciation outside this circle that they really deserve.

The inescapable character of Rudolf Steiner's argumentation in these works escapes the reader when he does not want to actually create the reasoning himself, which is more than just *thinking along* with it. On the one hand, this *will* to think is a lot harder for us people living now, weakened as we are because we have given up thinking for the passivity of following movies, television programmes and computer games etc. We have become more submissive in our thinking than ever before. On the other hand, the 'licence to think whatever we want', which means the absence of limits set by faith and tradition, is also greater than ever before. We can now engage this free, unprejudiced attitude of mind, which we have in our thinking, more than ever, in order to achieve a resurrection of strength in our thinking. In so doing, we overcome doubt which clings to weakened thinking.

Of the greatest importance in our time is that we become aware of the *different* soul processes that we call *thinking*. Steiner says: 'I contrast it (whatever I do not myself produce) with myself as something *the existence of which is independent of me*. It comes to meet me'. By contrast: 'For he observes something (thinking) which *he himself produces*.'

We must learn to make a distinction between the part of our life of thought which comes about beyond our will, and learn to stop calling this part 'thinking' – the whole of *associative* thinking is thus to be eliminated from the concept 'thinking' – and that part of our inner thought life which we bring to life *ourselves* as concepts and conceptual connections, which we may indeed call thinking, because it *is* thinking.

We discover then that in cognising everything else in the world, we are confronted by what we have not worked on creatively. Either we have not worked on something creatively at all (we have not worked consciously at the creation of Nature), or else we have worked consciously at it only *partially* (for example, in creating a work of art, we are unable to follow the process into our muscles which complete the work physically).

Rudolf Steiner shows how in cognising our own thinking we find ourselves in quite another situation because here not a single unknown element or any element that does not belong to us mingles in with the process of cognition. Then we can say with Rudolf Steiner: In thinking we keep the worldprocess at its tip, where we have to be there, if

116

something should come out.

The danger of endless regression, or going round in a circle, only threatens if we want to judge thinking abstractly again, from outside, as if it belonged to everything else which comes about beyond our will, as 'thing-in-itself'. If we learn to perceive thinking *as inner activity*, we pull it into our field of perception, into which it is never otherwise taken.

Initially, we cannot but observe thinking afterwards over and over again: we think and point our concentration at the thought afterwards. Subsequently, we can learn to point our attention to the thinking process, rather than to the content which thinking is addressing. We keep on doing both actions – thinking and then observing the thinking process – one after the other in time. One experiences how in this thinking, which is always thinking in mental representations, one cannot *be conscious of oneself in thinking in the present* - at first, there are mental representations of the content, and then mental representations of the process.

Only at the point of transition between not thinking and thinking, where one experiences oneself consciously as the initiator of thinking, lies the moment of absolute *presence* of mind (Geist), of being conscious of oneself in the present. Here at this point the I is *universalis ante rem, in re* and *post rem* at the same time. Here one breaks through the reflecting life of mental representations because one enters the concrete will life while fully maintaining the process of conscious thinking. Here it is not possible to make mental representations, one can only *be* thinking, willing. One enters the *unrepresentational*. Here the idea is reality, the material is spiritual; here going in a circle gives transcendence, describing is understanding. Here the I is the world, the world is the I.

In the 'Philosophy of Freedom' and his other epistemological works, Steiner proceeds from the life of mental representations – by cognising that life thoroughly – to the point where thinking and thought are one. The experience of this unification is not described explicitly in these works. Consequently, a real breaking through the life of mental representations can occur when one works intensively with these books – but it cannot be abstractly understood from the text. The I-experience occurs, but is not described as such.

In a later lecture and summary of the lecture Steiner does speak about this experience as follows:

From 'Philosophy and Anthroposophy', 17-8-1908:[16]

"Thus, epistemologically, we have the fundamental sentence: "that also in pure thinking a point is reachable in which reality and subjectivity fully touch each other, where man experiences reality." When he puts himself at that point and fructifies his thinking so that this thinking emerges from that point out of itself, then he grasps things from the inside. Therefore, in the I that is cognised through a pure act of thought and also created at the same time, there is something through which we penetrate the boundary that for everything else has to be set between form and matter."

In this lecture Steiner completes the Aristotelian concepts of form and matter through the I-philosophy of Fichte, through which he finds the triad I *ante rem*, I *in re* and I *post rem*.

The I-experience is the point where reality and subjectivity fully coincide. If one becomes strong at this point, one finds the possibility to direct one's reality-thinking to everything else while maintaining this I-experience. One no longer thinks oneself, but thinks reality. Thinking steps out of itself and grasps things from the inside. From this point we can find the transition to the next chapter: Science.

SCIENCE

THINKING ABOUT THOUGHT

How do we build the bridge between thinking which understands itself and the truthful understanding of everything else? We have demonstrated how doubt in thinking itself is overcome. With this victory, thinking has lost its abstract character and has taken on the character of concrete reality. In our own I we have found the artist who is creative in the substance that belongs to the I – thinking. Because of this we have a thorough understanding of what comes into being when we think.

When we start to research *how* we actually think when we pursue science, it can become clear where the causes of the abstract character of this science lie. We then find how, from this abstraction, doubt in the results of this science emerges. We do not look at how it should be, but how it *is*.

Modern science was born at a time where Copernicus proved that 'not everything turns around the earth', as had been thought up to then in the Ptolemaic world view, but that 'everything turns around the sun' – heliocentric astronomy. This discovery had great consequences for the experience of the meaning of the human being in the universe. The human being had to start to look at himself as a meaningless speck of dust in the great Universe. How could the thinking of this speck of dust have any significance in the Universe? On the other hand, it brought the human being to take a look at himself; he began to think self-reflexively and to put himself into perspective.

Then arose the great influence on science of Sir Francis Bacon, who made the case for an empirical science. The human being had to learn to exclude himself completely from the act of knowing – all subjectivity had to disappear - and learn to surrender to what nature herself has to say to him. For this, he needed to 'put nature to the question', according to Bacon, by forcing her into the straitjacket of the experiment, which is a torture, in order to force her give up her secrets. The human being had to rule nature completely according to the principle: knowledge is power.

Subsequently, Kant laid the epistemological foundation for modern science by basing this foundation on the following premise: an absolutely certain system of cognition is only possible when this is built up from synthetic *a priori* judgments, that is to say, compounded judgments (where the predicate is added to the subject) which are formed independently of any experience whatsoever. Kant thus made certain demands as to the form of cognition, if this cognition was to be a secure knowing.

We do not intend to work in that way in what follows. We do not want to put down a prior list of demands and then begin research if these demands are satisfied; we want to do the research first and then draw conclusions from the research.

MATHEMATICAL THINKING

How do we find the entrance to the world outside with our thinking? How can we extend our own thinking beyond ourselves to a thinking of the outside world?

First, we form a mathematical concept, and we shall see how we can still stay totally within our own thinking, and yet we no longer have only our own thinking as object. We are not thinking about our own thinking anymore, and neither are we yet thinking about something outside of us.

We formed the concept of the circle earlier. Then we only did this in order to provide a content for our thinking, so that we could activate our thinking. Now we want to try to see how we form the content, but at the same time we want to observe the thinking process. Thus we think the concept of the circle again.

As children we observed many circles and recognised them before we learned about the lawfulness of circles in maths lessons in school. But once we know this of lawfulness, we can keep on abstracting imagined circles and form the common concept of the circle within our thinking. This concept contains all the possible circles which one can ever meet in life. The common abstract concept of the circle thus contains more than circles which are observed or imagined, but also less than these, because the being of the circle, as far as it is inwardly thought of abstractly, does not actually come to life, it does not appear as a particular circle.

Let us go through this whole process. The concept of the circle is expressed in the words: "a circle is the mathematical area delineated by points in a plane, all of which are equidistant from the middle point of the area". Understanding this concept gives us the being of the circle if we are able to think this concept totally free of mental representations. Then we have a concept in our mind which contains nothing from anything else in the world, which thus lives totally in our own thinking. It *is*, however, in its content not only no longer our own thinking, but it is already a concept outside the concept of thinking itself.

In the mathematical concept we thus have a concept, which lives totally in itself, but which already points to everything, without carrying into itself observations and imaginations from everything else. We find a purified concept, a pure thinking free of perception and imagination, but which is no longer purely the concept of thinking. This forming of mathematical concepts is a process that we can carry out totally inside ourselves; thinking is here based completely on itself.

If we now look into this process we find besides the discovered, chosen concept of the circle also *how* we proceed in forming the concept. We find not only the content of the concept, but also the meaning of the forming of mathematical thinking. It is a pure thinking, in which we no longer think about thinking, nor do we think yet about everything else. For this discovery we thank our trained capacity to look at *how* we think.

After finding the circle as an essential concept, and

discovering the importance of pure mathematical think-ing, we can also point our attention to the process of understanding the definition in which the determination is expressed.

How do we understand the definition: "a circle is the mathematical area delineated by points in a plane, all of which are equidistant from the middle point of the area"? When we submit such a definition to further research, we see that it indeed expresses a simple concept, but that this concept 'circle' can only be understood with the help of other concepts. If we wish to understand the words in the definition, we must have at our disposal categories of elementary concepts. In our thinking there is a mechanism which enables us to differentiate the words, so that the light of understanding illumines the definition. Saying the words of the definition out loud does not supply us with the concept.

In the definition we are already using another definition: a mathematical area is a figure F which fulfils the following two conditions:

1. all the points of F have a similar quality;
2. each point which has this quality is a point of F."

Thus we can clarify the concept of the circle as follows: all the points of the geometrical figure in the flat plane, which we call circle, have a certain *relation* – equidistance – to a point in this flat plane.

When we have now understood this definition and have formed the concept of the circle thanks to this definition which we have understood, than we can construct a particular circle from the being 'circle', and make it appear either in our imaginative life or on paper.

When we observe ourselves thoroughly while constructing the circle, we see that we are inwardly *measuring* throughout the process: measuring is the determining of a *quantitative relation in space.* In this case of a general lawfulness – the quantity is not determined, we do not name a *particular* distance between the points of the circumference and the centre, but we apply an undetermined quantity (the length, the radius), a particular relationship (equidistance), and a specific spatial condition (the two-dimensional, flat plane). It is *geometry* that we are dealing with here, and we are able to do this because in our thinking we apply specific categories such as space, relation and quantity, which are not particular and which only receive their particularity in the world of the experience. The categories are the form; the experiences provide the content.

When, with Kant, we subsequently contend that these forms in thinking are only ordering principles which organise perceptions and do not go further than that, then we underestimate our formal thinking. For the perceived circle is a rigid, coagulated example of that which in thinking is endlessly mobile and includes all possible circles - the being of the circle, the *concept.* We cannot simply state that it is not possible to experience this concept, which is constructed purely internally, and that this would not be based on experience.

The concept is not a reflection of the outer, sensory experience of that one coagulated circle; but it is indeed possible to observe the living, moving concept of the circle, when we have trained ourselves to perceive our own thinking process. When we thus add the experience of our own thinking to the totality of possible experiences, the demand of Kant for the independence of any experience (if knowing is to be certain) does not apply. It is precisely certainty in thinking that we have found through the *experience* of that part of knowing which Kant calls 'a priori' and which arises beyond experience of everything else.

We shall seek to clarify our findings by forming another geometrical concept. We shall work the other way round now and start from a geometrical rule, without naming the figure yet. The rule states: the figure F is a geometrical place of points, in which the sum of distances to two fixed points, the foci, is constant; the straight line through these two foci is the large axis, and a small axis divides the big axis perpendicularly in two; the length of the large axis is equal to the constant sum of the distances of the points in figure F to the foci. When we now have this rule, we must understand it first, before we are able to form the concept which comes into being from it. If the rule does not call up an imagination inside us directly – if we are, for example, mathematically inclined - or if speaking out loud the name of the figure does not directly make the mental picture come to our imagination – then we can, thanks to our understanding of the definition, construct the figure, apart from the imagination of it, because we do not have that yet. Only when the construction is made do we also have the imagination of the figure and the concept of the figure in its full reality, because the abstract concept comes into

129

being in an imagination of the figure. When we abstract from this imagination again, and form the concept again which contains all the imaginations of the figure, we find the pure, sense-free concept. We find the figure illustrated on page 131.

Here too, in order to come to the construction, we apply quantitative relations in a spatial sense: we *measure*. With the construction on paper we even apply *specific* quantities, to come to the particular figure which we want to put down on paper. Because we have worked from the determination to the name, we see that *without using any internal memory pictures* - exclusively using our comprehension - we come to the construction of the ellipse through thinking. It would even be possible without putting the figure down on paper; using all the forces at our disposal, we can also construct it totally internally.

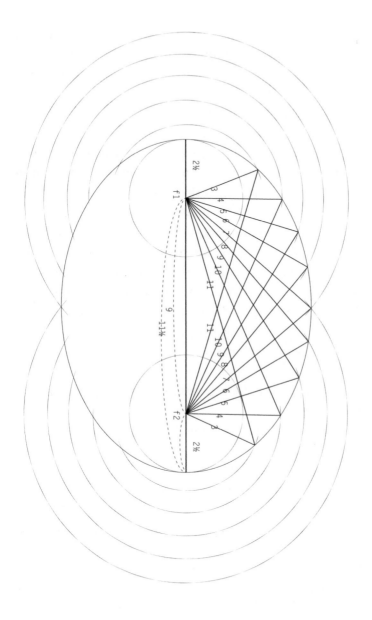

Fig. 3

Here too we find a mobile concept, which contains all possible ellipses, contrary to the one fixed form of ellipse, which we can observe here or there with our senses. According to Kant, we can never reach the heart of things when we bring together experience and form. When, however, we learn to experience form that has been brought into movement, then we have found the starting point where the heart of things lives in endlessly mobile form, which becomes experience.

Nevertheless, we can grow old without ever having learned a definition such as this, of, for example, the ellipse, while yet being able to recognise the ellipse as a figure and name. A contemplation of both possibilities of knowing sheds light on 'learning by heart' versus learning by understanding.

Summarizing, we can say:

– We can recognise a geometrical figure without understanding it.
– We can only *understand* the determination of a concept, and construct a geometrical figure, apart from any mental picture.
– We can carry out a mathematical thinking exercise, even an algebra equation without the help of mental representations of the outside world, thus completely image-free. In algebra the (aristotelian) category 'space' is irrelevant, and thinking operates exclusively according to the categories of 'quantity' and 'relation'.
– Mathematical thinking is a pure thinking, a sense-free thinking, insofar as it moves purely internally in the

non-specified, mobile categories of 'quantity', 'relation' and 'space'.

Here in mathematical thinking we find the transition from thinking about thinking to thinking about everything else in life, because we are *no longer* thinking about thinking and *nor are we thinking* about everything else in life, as far as it concerns the world of the sensory impressions and imaginations. When we experience mathematical thinking, we know – as in thinking about thinking – that we are the thinker ourselves, that we are creating ourselves, that what comes to life, comes into being from our own creative power. To become aware of this means to understand the human being's need for a mathematical understanding of the world of sense experience, of nature. For we then find the connection of our own creating thinking with natural laws, and thus we find satisfaction in knowing.

But when we then see what the consequences are of this desire to understand nature mathematically, we find that they are extreme. We see that we have learned to understand the world in formulae, which have squeezed the life out of her.

To illustrate this, I shall give several simple examples from contemporary scientific thinking. First, an example from physiology:
By means of our eyes, we observe a lively, colourful world. In seeing colour contrasts, we also see boundaries, figures, forms. We see images. Compare the self-research of the artistic experience of the colours around us in the world,

to a statement about seeing colours from a physiology textbook, in a chapter about physiological optics:[17]

"As long as one is describing the physical phenomena of light, one can only speak of different forms of speed, wavelength, frequency, and therefore for every medium of refractive index e.g. in relation to a vacuum. Physically, it makes no sense to give the name of a colour to a particular frequency which we would see when we see this light with our normal eyes at a sufficiently great intensity of light and which would then affect our brain. And yet, the name of the colour is almost always used instead of frequency (or when necessary instead of wavelength in a vacuum or in the air) under the above-mentioned circumstances for the sake of brevity."

Following this quote there is printed an image of a table in which the emission lines are named in the light spectrum with the corresponding wave lengths and colours.

Now it is in no way my intention to cast doubt on the scientific value of these insights. Rather, here it is about the *experience* of a mathematical penetration of reality, namely, that however great and valuable it may be, it always leads to a diminution of the experience of reality.

A great part of physiological optics is dedicated to the forming of an image on the retina. The true function of the eye, however, lies in seeing *colours*. This happens because of the rods and cones in the retina. Cones provide for seeing in bright light, rods for seeing in the dark. Thus, scientists have found differences in the eye functions for seeing in the light and in the dark. They find sensitivity curves, photochromatic intervals and the like, but the actual seeing in light and seeing in darkness remains a mystery. It is expressed in formulae and conceived of statically. But the dynamics of seeing can not be put in curves; they escape knowledge. We even forget that there *is* a dynamic. Life itself escapes knowledge.

As a second example, I would like to present for the reader's reflection several approaches of the colour doctrine of Newton, Huygens, Maxwell, and others on the one hand, and that of Goethe on the other hand. Newton orders the different colours according to their wavelength and frequency vibration and comes to *quantitative* values for the different colour *qualities*. He considers light to consist of particles, which have an unequal refractive index, according to their different accelerations at the interface. Huygens explains the difference in the refractive index as being due to differences in wave length, in frequency. In the 19th century Maxwell developed the electromagnetic theory of light, and in the 20th century came the quantum theory of light (Max Planck, Albert Einstein *et al*).

Contrary to these physical light theories is the research of Goethe, which tries to hold to the qualitative nature of light and the different colours. He researches the combined action between light and darkness and finds that different colour qualities arise as a result of variations in the meeting of light with darkness. Blue comes into being when light meets a strong material resistance – darkness; yellow comes into being when light meets only little material resistance. From this qualitative penetration into the reality of colours, he comes to a description of the sensory-moral effect of colours, the moral quality of colour experienced with the eye, which has as much objective value as the quantitative values.

J.W. von Goethe:[18]
"Since colour occupies so important a place in the series of elementary phenomena, filling as it does the limited circle assigned to it with fullest variety, we shall not be surprised to find that it brings on an effect on the sense of the eye - by means of which it acts on the mind and through its mediation on emotions in their most elementary appearances, without any relation to the nature and form of the substance on whose surface they appear - if it appears simple a specific, in combination a partly harmonious, but always a decided and significant effect, that touches the moral aspect. Hence, colour considered as an element of art, may be made subservient to the highest aesthetical ends.

People experience a great delight in colour, generally. The eye requires it as much as it requires light. We have only to remember the refreshing sensation we experience if, on a cloudy day, the sun illumines a single portion of the scene before us and displays its colours. That healing powers were ascribed to coloured gems may have arisen from the deep feelings of this indefinable pleasure.

The colours that we see on objects are not qualities entirely strange to the eye; the organ is thus not merely habituated to the impression; no, it is always predisposed to produce colour of itself, and experiences a sensation of delight if something analogous to its own nature is offered to it from without; if its susceptibility is distinctly determined towards a given state."

Newton and Huygens exclude qualitative experience from their science, but to Goethe it is an indispensable element; however, he nevertheless lays claim to objectivity in the results of his research.

These simple scientific examples are given in order to enable the reader to *experience* the scientific mode of knowing. It is not scientific *content* that is key here, but the *process*, performing internally oneself that which is continually operative in scientific work, and which has to be *known* if one wants to know what use science is to him.

In the chapter 'Philosophia' we proved the reliability of thinking about thinking. We can trust thinking in itself because we know through and through how we do it, we create it ourselves continuously; we would not be able to create the content if we ourselves *were not the capacity for comprehension of concepts* from which we make the content come into being. But has this thinking which is aware of itself also a certain, recognisable relation to everything else in life? Do we live, while thinking' about everything else, in the real being of it? Or does thinking remain a dubious semblance in this process of cognition, which may be called the science of everything else in life?

In mathematical thinking we have found a way of thinking which is no longer thinking about thinking, but which has a content, different from thinking itself. Equipped with mathematical concepts, with which we feel profoundly connected, we can subsequently penetrate reality, the nature of everything else, and understand it. Thus we find a connection between our own understanding and reality.

When, for example, we analyse light quantitatively in the Newtonian manner, do we gain a connection to the true being of light? Does the satisfaction which we feel when we have understood light quantitatively also give us the satisfaction that are in touch with the full truth of reality?

Anyone who looks at himself carefully in this whole process of knowing will have to admit: in mathematical thinking I find a quantitative thinking, even a spatially quantitative thinking, which I can construct from within myself. The penetrating of a phenomenon such as light with this quantitative thinking brings understanding of light closer, but I retain only a schema; the qualitative *experiencing* of the light as I had experienced it 'naively', no longer plays a role. I understand quantitatively, but I lose the quality.

Therefore, we can do no more than admit to ourselves that we do not experience full reality in this form of science; we only understand schematically. If we have found a truth at all, it is a partial truth.

That casts doubt on the reliability of our sense observations and our thoughts about them; it casts doubt on the possibility for truth in thinking and knowing. What we see of light and colour with our eyes, is that really also present in nature, or is there a schematic world of moving particles consistent with mathematical laws and do our senses conjure this world into a world of colour, sound, warmth? Which is 'right' - our mathematical thinking, or our senses? Or are both only indications of a reality, access to the full reality though is denied us?

EMPIRISM

Thus far, we have sought to find the transition from thinking about thinking to thinking about everything else. As the first step in this search, we have thought mathematically, and found a thinking which we can produce completely by ourselves, like thinking about thinking, but which, however, has a different subject from thinking itself. In so far as we can find mathematical laws in everything else in the world, which is not constructed by us, we feel unifiedwith this 'everything else in the world', even if we lose the experience of the full reality of it.

Diametrically opposite this mathematical thinking, we find a totally different form of scientific practice, namely, empirical science. This takes its stand directly in 'everything else in the world' and allows its results to be led by experiments. Here, thinking produces no concepts from itself, but lets its procedure be determined totally by natural laws observed in everything except thinking. In this approach, truth is only accepted when the results are found by experiment, or when a hypothesis which is formed in thinking as a presumed truth, can be confirmed by an experiment. In empirical science we make our thinking content comply with everything else in the world; we try to discipline our thinking content strictly so that it becomes a reflection of the outer world (everything else). The outer world is the teacher and thinking is the student. It is of the utmost importance to be introspective here also, as an experiment, in order to learn to experience what we *do* when we carry out empirical scientific work.

In empirical science, thinking is determined by observation. The daily work of the doctor in his consulting room is an example of empirical scientific work. The patient presents a certain disorder pattern and presents the observation and thinking of the doctor with a riddle. What is going on? In order to answer this question, the doctor has to be a good observer - listening, watching, tapping, feeling. A good doctor approaches his patient without prejudice, without hypothesis, but lets his thinking be determined on the one hand by what he has observed, and on the other hand by the concepts and judgments which he has made his own by his study and experience. These become, so to say, awakened by unprejudiced observation. The capability of the doctor consists in his ability to be unprejudiced in his observation on the one hand, and his ability to let his thinking be awakened by this observation on the other hand. It is a thinking that is rich in medical scientific content. This scientific thinking content lives in the 'form' of categories such as place, time, suffering, etc.

The general categories (time, place, etc.) have taken on a specific scientific character in accordance with the doctor's specialist studies, and he approaches his patient with this specific pattern of thinking. In relation to the patient this specific pattern becomes general again and only becomes specific after the doctor has made his observations. The final judgment – diagnosis – is mostly determined in the form of cause and effect, and thus in the category of causality.

When we attend to this whole process, we experience ourselves as thinker between observation on the one hand, and on the other hand, the world of the already existing thinking content. The more dynamically one can, as thinker, link the one thing to the other, the purer his science is.

One can see Sir Francis Bacon as the founder of modern empirical science. He had a *goal* with this form of science, namely, the human being's mastery of nature. The student must finally become more than the teacher. On the one hand, thinking must endure a kind of asceticism - because it abstains from personal preconceptions and learns to adjust itself totally to observation. On the other hand, it must use the power obtained thereby – because one does obtain that! – to become a master over nature: knowledge must become power, with which one teaches nature to obey man.

For Bacon, thinking only has a systematizing function; it produces nothing from itself, but receives its content totally from observation. In mathematical thinking we have found a way of thinking which is in conflict with this view. This mathematical thinking weaves and lives totally within itself and is *more* than a reflection of the observed truth, because it is able to think a circle, which encloses *all* possible circles. We will never find such a circle in observed reality; there we always find specific fixed examples.

Now, Goethe had this quality of mathematical thinking - namely, the ability to discover primal phenomena, all-embracing concepts, which contain all possible appearances but which never themselves fully appear in the sense world and are yet always evident in that world through a variety of forms – and he carried it through in thinking on the basis of sensory observations of living nature. Therefore, he educated his thinking so that he was able to observe purely with his full attention, but without an already formed judgment or one that was forming as he observed. But we must certainly not imagine that he turned off his *thinking* while he observed. On the contrary, his thinking followed his sensory observation very openly and powerfully, full of inner will and activity, but without judgment, and perceived the primal phenomenon just *because of* this thinking, *in* this thinking, on the basis of observation, but not *from* the observation. Goethe received this primal phenomenon from the spirit, from his individual, thus not subjective, spirit. The spirit of the human being Goethe and living reality resonated together and found each other in true reality. Whoever wants to follow him finds the possibility to understand everything else in life *without loosing his full experience of reality.*.

When we experientially know how we work scientifically, we learn at the same time to experience what meaning knowledge has for daily life, for every day of our lives we are applying the categories of cause and effect, quantity and relation. This is how we raise our children. Because we always understand their expressions as 'why/how' questions, they learn always to ask: 'why?'

In this way we cultivate thinking patterns, which unfold automatically over and over again later in their lives, without the thinker being aware of what takes place and without him wondering if the question of cause and effect is the most important one.

Thus we rediscover the human need for a mathematical understanding, the need to understand daily life in terms of quantitative relations. Quantitative assessments permeate our thinking and judgments, and also penetrate the non-quantitative aspects of our lives. How much we want to 'measure' our qualities and compare them with those of other people! Measuring and weighing ourselves compared to others plays an important role in maintaining our own self-esteem. Thus, thinking patterns give rise to errors in thinking, because one is not aware either of one's own thinking or of the lawfulness that rules in one's thinking.

MEDITATION

In the chapter 'Philosophia' I have shown how we can find ourselves as I, by starting to think consciously and experience the initiator – the I. Now we shall look for the transition from thinking about thinking, or rather the perceiving of thinking, the consciously being present in thinking, to thinking about everything else in the world, but as a *real transition*. In the chapter 'Philosophia' we questioned thinking itself. We had to create a concept because we needed an example of thought-creation, so that we could try to perceive it while acting. Here though we want to find out if it is also possible to find the full truth of 'everything else' with the same certainty. The ability that we have developed in philosophy, namely, the capacity to observe oneself as a thinking being - we want to take this with us in this transition.

Here now we find the origin of doubt about our capacity to find the truth in thinking about everything else in the world. Namely, as soon as we turn from thinking about thinking and open our senses to everything else, the possibility to keep thinking about thinking escapes us. We fill our mind with mental representations of everything else and lose the self we found in thinking. We may stand as I facing the world, but our I is transformed into mental representations *of* the world, and we have no certainty if these mental representations provide us with truth about the world. Is this world actually as we represent it to ourselves? If we can carry mathematical laws into these mental representations, we at least have the satisfying *memory* of having constructed these concepts ourselves. The creating activity itself is lost and becomes a memory. When we search for causality in our mental representations, we experience our dependence on our observations in this matter; on the other hand, we experience the danger of arbitrariness in our judgments because we make the causal link from out of ourselves.

How do we find the way out of *this* doubt? We have seen how doubt in knowing everything other than thinking arises because the reality of everything else escapes us. We can *perceive* in a static state, but are not able to *think* the origin of things.

In thinking about thinking certainty arises because we can learn to *perceive* thinking by initiating it ourselves; we create it ourselves, we *think* it ourselves. Both these certainties in thinking escape us when we turn to everything other than thinking; we then experience thinking *utterly as a semblance;* we no longer perceive it. Consequently, our own creative activity slips our mind too.

If we want to maintain with open senses the consciousness of our thinking as creative activity during the act of cognising anything other than thinking, we shall have to learn always to *initiate and watch thinking consciously while imagining, while forming our mental representations.* Only then can we know if thinking has anything to do with the real world, and if yes, *what precisely.*

Here opens the abyss before which the modern cognitive process stands. There is a yawning gulf between the I and the world. In knowing, we lose ourselves as thinkers, we only have reflections of the world inside our I, and with that we have lost all certainty in knowing.

Doubt is the abyss.

In order to be able to ascertain the value of knowing and the possibility of finding the truth in knowing, we shall only be able to bridge this abyss, if we can awaken a pure human characteristic, which slumbers in every human being as a germ, like a seed that has not been sown, and which does not come into being naturally. Just as a seed is not able to sprout if it is not sowed in good soil, the human being is not able to develop his pure human quality if he does not cultivate this slumbering germ.

When he only *uses* this germ, without taking care of it, he acts like a farmer who uses all his wheat to grind bread, without saving any to be used as seed to sow for the next harvest.

We have found certainty in thinking because we have learned to see ourselves as thinker, as creator, as the initiator of thinking.

Now, in cognising anything besides thinking, we have lost this certainty again because sense impressions ('everything else') are so overwhelming that we are no longer aware of ourselves as thinkers. On the one hand, we experience the content of our mental representations as reflections of reality; on the other hand, we doubt the truth of them because we also experience that these reflections bubble up *from ourselves, and not from the reality that is observed.*

We shall have to strengthen thinking, the instrument of the 'Oh Man, know yourself' which is at the same time the object of self-knowledge, the germ of our being human and that area where we live completely consciously, so that it will be able to maintain itself when we direct our power of attention at anything else in the world besides thinking.

The path to achieve this is the path of *meditation*.

This word meditation is a word which cannot be assigned to an unambiguous concept. It has become a buzzword and covers all those inner and outer activities which are practised a little more intensely and longer than usual. When someone does not ignore nature, but lets it sink in a little more, one could call it 'meditation' in the sense the word is often used nowadays. Observing one's own thinking life, one's own inner emotions, can also be called meditation, even if it exclusively concerns observing the *content* of one's thinking or feeling.

Here I want to develop a concept to which I shall give the name 'meditation'. From this point onwards in this book, 'meditation' will be understood to refer to this concept.
Besides this vagueness about the meaning of the word meditation, this word and the commonly used concept of it has an effect on people which could be called unscientific and unrelated to the concept 'science'. Meditation is commonly taken these days to mean transcendence, mysticism, religious fulfilment. Here, however, meditation is used in order to gain control over the *instrument* for science - namely, *thinking*.

148

Rudolf Steiner established this method (meditation) for the development of thinking, the instrument of science as the foundation of his later spiritual scientific work. The world only wanted to see this spiritual work, assessed it and generally banished it to the realm of mysticism. Science did not accept the significance of this method for humanity and for the development of the specifically human capability, scientific knowledge.

Which musician, for example, would call himself a pianist, who does not know the piano and how to play it? He has to have a thorough command of his instrument in order to play it so that what he plays is really *music* and not merely technique. Thus one can develop science from an ability into an art when one does not only know the instrument with which one practices science, thinking, but also masters it. By 'mastering' is not meant 'controlling', but being able to play the instrument from the inside out and experiencing it thoroughly. Only then can science become more than technique and at the same time no unclear, mystical, unaware affair. We maintain our clear, scientific state of mind; indeed, it is precisely *that* which we employ to make what is unaware aware.

A true scientist is not scared off by the word 'meditation' but is encouraged in his urge to research, to unlock a previously undiscovered area, namely, the area of the instrument of science itself. If we can prove indisputably to him – through the presenting to him the possibility to carry out and test this research *himself* in his own activity - that meditation is the right way to achieve his goal, he will seize it, whatever he has thought about meditation up to then. All the research results described here are to be tested and are repeatable; but here it is up to each person to do the research and the proving for himself!

The development of the concept 'meditation'.

When we want to learn to observe and experience thinking in ourselves as a reality, a reality which is maintained in the face of overwhelming sense perception, we must learn to *stand still* in our thinking instead of being led by it.

The first thing we have to learn is to gain *control* over the waves of associative thinking. To this end, we choose an image or a text which does not call up associations and we give our total attention to this thought content. As in philosophical thinking, we initiate this content ourselves in full consciousness and we remain quite still in it. It must be a thought content which can be held as one thought and which can be surveyed in one thinking glance. It calls up no associations or memories whatsoever, so that the attention is not mingled with musings from one's own biography or with familiar ideas, even if they come from philosophical or scientific work. Here too, it is not mainly about the chosen content – though of course that does play a role – but about the process of learning to stand still in thinking.

If we want to find a thought content which does not call up associations or memory images, we can even take a thought from thinking about thinking, as we did in the

150

chapter Philosophia. We can, for example, look to the point where we initiate thinking, and subsequently hold on to this point as a thinking concentration. It will be clear that in this content nothing is allowed in from the life of the senses. Another possibility is the concentration on a symbol, i.e. an image, which is built of contents derived from the senses, but in which the constructed image as such is not to be found in the sense world. In world literature we can find a wealth of such images. For example, there is the 'rod of Asclepius', which is derived from the staff of Mercury, which points out the path from earth to heaven in a perpendicular line, the path of development which the human kind has to walk if he is not to be thrown off track. The snake which slides around the perpendicular symbolizes the errors we make, our deviations from the right path.

Fig. 4

Now this concentration in the midst of the unquiet, inner and outer life that we lead, plagued as it is with burdens of all

151

kinds, will take a great deal of effort. Associations want to disturb our thinking all the time; they want to take the place of our willed thinking. Again and again we must strongly avert this associative thinking and direct ourselves to our chosen content. It is the very effort that we make in doing this that strengthens the power of our thinking. Here lies the difference with Eastern paths of development: westerners must go through thinking, through the intellect, at the cost of great effort and exertion, while the Oriental stands still before thinking, in devotion to the divine All, or tries to ward off associative thinking by overcoming the intellect.

This meditative exercise, which requires effort with every practice, is not aimed at a certain result but is about the *activity*. It is not a particular aim, but a means to *overcome thinking in abstractions* by strengthening the abstract thinking, because willpower is brought into thinking. As long as we cannot maintain thinking as experience in our observation of everything else, thinking remains abstract in the strict sense of the word; we experience it as appearances detached from reality, indeed, we can even experience it as an *impediment* to entering this reality.

Learning to stand still in one's thinking day after day, even year after year, will lead to this experience: up to now I was guided by the stream of thinking and experienced thinking as content, but not the stream itself. Now I stand still in the stream, it is not about the ongoing content; I experience now around me, inside me, *that* power that *moves* thinking. Through learning to be motionlessness I experience movement. At first, I observe this movement only during meditation. Opening my senses overwhelmes my thinking power. But with the increasing strength of my thinking in the manner described above *then* the moment comes when I *also* observe this thinking power with a concentrated use of the senses. *This* is the greatest moment, when one *sees that* the abyss between oneself and the world is only there in the abstract semblance of thinking. The developed inner activity in the meditative life has led to one's being able to perceive, to feel tangibly even, the thought-*power* which produces the thinking *content*. This power one feels to be living in one's own thinking, but *at the same time* as the thinking creative power that is actually active in nature. One *watches* the real creative thinking that underlies the world; one watches the human thinking which underlies that part of the world that is of human origin and has a static character (architecture, art); one watches the divine thinking which works livingly in nature as the ever mobile, growing and forming power.

One has *not* understood the whole content of creation but one watches the thinking power which is a real creative power in the world, and which on the other hand *infuses and illumines* the concepts in the human mind. The moving, streaming, thinking power is the union between the self with its concepts and the world with its natural laws, because it *is* both. The thinking power lives as reality in the world's natural laws and in the mind's concepts at the same time. In human consciousness the world meets itself.

If we stand in the world with opened senses and perceive, and if we are able to feel the thinking processes as power during this observing, we will then for the first time 'see' the meaning, the share that this thinking has in the process of observation. If we observe from our 'normal' consciousness, we experience perception of the sense world as a ready-made image which we experience ourselves as confronting.

If we observe with a thinking power that is 'upright' and 'awakened', only then do we notice how it has always escaped us that thinking is interwoven in sense perceptions. We experience the thinking power *in* the observation and watch how we have always been thinking while observing, even when we were of the opinion that *we were exclusively perceiving and not thinking.* If we are aware of our thinking power, we are able to pull it out of observing for a moment and experience then how sense perception is an absolute chaos of impressions, without any single differentiations. We can only differentiate red from green when we *think* the observed red and green. And we realize that this developing thinking process *in* thinking that we have developed already as a child, *is the living part, within our consciousness,* of a reality which, even without our activity, is already as differentiated as we render it through our thinking. This thinking observation which every human being engages in without knowing it, becomes for us, if it is cognised, a living in reality. Our powerful, mobile thinking lives in things; the living thinking that lives in things moves in us. And in this living mobile thinking we carry a form principle which categorizes and differentiates the otherwise formless matter.

This form principle differentiates itself in concepts with which we only appear to confront the observed world. In reality however, this differentiation really lives in the world. This form principle, which differentiates itself in common concepts, is expressed by Aristotle *as describing the science of the technique of thinking* in its ten conceptual categories. These ten categories (*substance, quality, quantity, space, time, relation, position, having, doing and suffering*) are the differentiated form with which we must face matter and which therefore are always *true*, because they also really give to matter the form that we observe. We, however, do not derive this form principle only from the observed reality; we carry it *a priori* inside us; on the one hand, this thinking power illumines these categories *a priori* and on the other hand, it lives in sense perceptions. Our thinking *power* makes us cognizant of *union*, of 're-ligio' (re-binding) with the creative powers of the world.

Here lies the problem with which every epistemology sees itself presented: the conceptual categories live *a priori* inside us; we do not derive them from the observed reality, but fill them with content, which we derive from that observed reality. But even if these categories are *a priori* present as form principles, yet they are also the true form of the matter outside our thinking, i.e. in the reality of everything else in life they are the true form. The form principle *comes to life* in us and shows us that it is not a schematizing mechanism, but the ability of the human being to participate in the stream of world events through thinking. The human being can find reality in his ideas and in (outer) reality the idea and he can therefore rise above one-sided perception or one-sided concepts.

In normal consciousness thinking power is numbed, we experience ourselves with our thinking inside ourselves and outside the world, over against the world. Thus it escapes us that the form which lives within ourselves is at the same time the form living outside us.

If the thinking-*power* starts to speak, we *see* that this power lively forms reality and at the same time forms our concepts and illumines them. The form that lives in our thinking as categories is *really* that which in our spirit participates in the world process, even though we do not derive it from that world, but from our spirit. Through the speaking thinking-power, the conceptual categories become the key to the door that separates spirit and world.

THINKING IN PERCEPTION

In order to experience clearly how the thinking-power lives both *in* the perceiving and *in* the understanding, we shall refer to two quotes: first, a quote from "Die Rätsel der Philosophie" (The Riddles of Philosophy) by Rudolf Steiner[19], in order to further illustrate the thinking power *in* sense-perception, and secondly, a quote from "Wissenschaft der Logik" (The Science of Logic, Part II) by Hegel[20] in order to cast more light on the thinking-power *in* the concept, in understanding.

Quote from "The Riddles of Philosophy" (Part II, Chapter VII):

"This impasse will be overcome only if in a spiritual way the fact is faced that, by its very nature, sense perception does not present a finished self-contained reality, but an unfinished, incomplete reality, or a half-reality, as it were. As soon as one presupposes that a full reality is gained through perceptions of the sensory world, one is forever prevented from finding the answer to the question: What has the creative mind to add to this reality in the act of cognition? By necessity one shall have to sustain the Kantian option: Man must consider his knowledge to be the inner product of his own mind; he cannot regard it as a process that is capable of revealing a true reality. If reality lies *outside* the soul, then the soul cannot produce anything that corresponds to this reality, and the result is merely a product of the soul's own organization.

The situation is entirely changed as soon as it is realized that the human soul does not deviate from reality in its creative effort for knowledge, but that prior to any cognitive activity the soul conjures up a world that is *not* real. Man is so placed in the world that by the nature of his being he changes things from what they really are. Hamerling is partly right when he says: 'Certain stimuli produce the odor within our organ of smell. The rose, therefore, has no fragrance if nobody smells it. . . . If this, dear reader, does not seem plausible to you, if your mind stirs like a shy horse when it is confronted with this fact, do not bother to read another line; leave this book and all others that deal with philosophical things unread, for you lack the ability that is necessary for this purpose, that is, to apprehend a fact without bias and to adhere to it in your thoughts.' How the sensory world *appears* when man is confronted with it, depends without a doubt on the nature of the soul. Does it not follow then that this appearance of the world is a *product of man's soul*? An unbiased observation shows, however, that the unreal character of the external sense world is caused by the fact that when man is directly confronted by things of the world, he suppresses something that really belongs to them. If he unfolds a creative inner life that lifts from the depths of his soul the forces that lie dormant in them, he adds something to the part perceived by the senses and thereby turns a half-reality to its entirety. It is due to the nature of the soul that, at its first contact with things, it *extinguishes* something that belongs to them. For this reason, things appear to the senses not as they are in reality but as they are modified by the soul. Their delusive character (or their mere appearance) is caused by the fact that the soul has deprived them of something that really belongs to them. Inasmuch as man does not merely observe things, he adds something to them in the process of knowledge that reveals their full reality. The mind does not add anything to things in the process of cognition that would have to be considered as an unreal element, but prior to the process of knowledge it has deprived these things of something that belongs to their true reality. It will be the task of philosophy to realize that the world accessible to man is an "illusion" *before it is approached in the process of cognition.* This process, however, leads the way toward a full understanding of reality. The knowledge that man creates during the process of cognition seems to be an inner manifestation of the soul only because he must, before the act of cognition, reject what comes from the nature of things. He cannot see at first the real nature of things when he encounters them in mere observation. In the process of knowledge he unveils what was first concealed. If he regards as a reality what he had at first perceived, he will now realize that he has added the results of his cognitive activity to reality. As soon as he recognises that what was apparently produced by himself has to be sought in the things themselves, that he merely failed to see it previously, he will then find that the process of knowing is a real process by which the soul progressively unites with world reality. Through it, it expands its inner isolated experience to the experience of the world."*

---

* (transl. Fritz C. A. Koelln, *The Riddles Of Philosophy,* Anthroposophic Press, Spring Valley, New York, 1973)

159

In this reasoning lies a point which is not so easy to follow, because one cannot prove the thought process for oneself. Consequently, there is the danger that the whole reasoning is dismissed as a fantastic theory, worthless to philosophy. The key point here is described in the following sentence from the quote:

"An unbiased observation shows, however, that the unreal character of the external sense world is caused by the fact that when man is directly confronted by things of the world, he suppresses something that really belongs to them."

Whereas up to this point the reasoning can be followed logically, here a result of self-observation is mentioned that one can easily put aside as fantasy, which would invalidate the whole argument. This is repeatedly the case with thinkers who have not developed thoughts *about* their thinking process, but who rather, have developed thoughts *out of* their thinking process. One can then do two things if one still wishes to follow their arguments and put them to a critical test. One can develop one's own ability of self-observation and subsequently strengthen it, in the manner described in this book so that one develops the ability to think and judge *out of* the thinking process *oneself*. One can, however, also make one's own life into the test, i.e. that one lives for a while in a questioning mode with regard to Steiner's reasoning about the character of the human soul, and that will mostly take quite a long time, it cannot be hastily surveyed in one thought. The first option produces the same result out of one's own experience; the second

160

method ultimately produces the experience of the result from unprejudiced research into that result. Both options call for patience and persistence, which are qualities that our hasty, modern 'knowledge-based society' does not foster. However, a rash acceptance of the research results of thinkers about reality such as Hegel and Steiner does them no justice, because they are the ones who, by the way they choose their words, call upon us to develop the patience and care which lead to right judgments.

The first path leads to an experience of the I as thinker, of the I as thought. Through the certainty we obtain in thinking, all doubt about the relationship between the I and thinking disappears. Experiencing this certainty makes the insecurity in cognising everything else in life appear all the more sharply. A strengthening, through meditation, of our thinking to the point where it becomes a power we can experience makes us aware of the position and meaning of thinking in our observation and understanding of everything else in life. Only then can we realise that the lack of experience of this thinking-power gives rise precisely to the error in cognition described by Rudolf Steiner - that our thoughts would be the products of our own souls and as such could not be ascribed to the outer world. Owing to the fact that normally, we exclusively experience our thoughts and not our *thinking* as observable activity, we keep on experiencing our thoughts as mere semblance, which is subject to doubt. But if, on the contrary, we find thinking itself in the process of cognition, we observe that thinking is the very thing which we extinguish in ourselves during our observation of the outer world, and that through this extinguishing, we can no longer experience ourselves as united with that outside world, but separated from it. We experience ourselves the reality of the results of the research described by Steiner.

The second path leads gradually to our *concurrence* with Steiner's description of reality, because by directing our attention again and again on the process of cognition, we gradually begin to sense that something escapes us in cognition, something that is actually the very thing that could give us certainty in cognition.

The ever stronger experience of alienation from reality in our observation of the world *and* of our satisfaction and feeling of unity with reality in our understanding through our conceptions brings us – not through security, but through the experience of impotence and insecurity – closer to that world which embraces both perception and concept, namely, thinking.

PREJUDICE AND HYPOTHESIS

We have overcome doubt in thinking about thinking; we have overcome it in finding thinking as a power, because we have seen that it is a universal power that is unifying inside and outside. We have found this powerful thinking as alive in all our sensory observations, interweaving with them. But how do we find the concept corresponding to this well-thought-out perception? After all, to come to science we have to combine our thinking perceptions with insights. Here again lies the possibility of error, because we are inclined to form *prejudices*. We shall first examine what a prejudice is and after that, move on to consider what *understanding* is.

We then have a prejudice when we approach the result of thinking perception with a self-made judgment which is already present in our mind before we observe attentively or one which we form during this observation. In order to track this process, a very delicate self-observation is needed, in order to be able to notice how a prejudice sneaks into a judgment, nests itself inside the judgment as if it was an effect of pure, attentive observation. Someone can be of the opinion that he approaches the world in an unprejudiced manner, but actually, unbeknownst to himself, gives the world his own pre-formed judgment.

In science nowadays a prejudiced approach to reality has even become the norm. Positing a hypothesis is just such a form of creating a prejudice. One is indeed willing to let

163

this prejudice be corrected by experiment, but one can not escape the fact that one makes it into a *habit* to construct a possible truth first oneself and then subsequently check it against reality. One underestimates thereby the secret preference one has for one's own pre-formed judgments, or prejudices, and as a result of this self-love, it is hard to let go of one's prejudices.

Whoever has once found the truth of thinking *sees* how the human being puts himself on the wrong track in conventional natural scientific thinking. One really sees the unity of the power of thinking in perception *and* understanding, and experiences the observational aspect of the power of thinking as *given*, and the understanding aspect of it as something that has to be *searched for*. Constructing the concepts *oneself* and combining them in judgments formed according to one's own caprices then becomes an activity which, because of its very nature, is contrary to the unifying character of the power of thinking.

In philosophy the truth of thinking about thinking can be found precisely by initiating thinking, forming concepts oneself, and in experiencing how the human being works creatively in thinking. Thus this thinking must be strengthened in itself, in meditation, in order to keep on noticing one's thinking when one practices science. *Then,* however, the human being has to be willing to abandon his own capricious forming of concepts and judgments and surrender his thinking-power fully to sense-perception (observation). In this fully attentive observation that is free of one's own prejudice and of hypotheses, in this thinking

164

observation full of devotion to the sense percept, in which the content of thinking is *exclusively* the fully attentive sensory observation, that one experiences as a living power, without a conceptual content, the congruent, true concept unites itself with the pure observation because the power of thinking which is active in observing sense percepts is the same power of thinking that creates one's internal concepts. One has no longer to invent judgments and concepts, but thinks them through this attentive observation.

Of course, one cannot perceive concepts which one has not yet already acquired through learning. The process of cognition has not become an effortlessly unfolding miracle; one has to make the concepts one's own through study. These acquired concepts light up in the cognitive process when they join with attentive sense-perception. Thus, one also sees what one does *not* yet know. When no concepts emerge during one's observation, one has to say: 'I don't know'.

Trust is awakened with the insight that observation (percept) and understanding (concept) are two sides of one and the same reality, and that by becoming active in thinking and learning to live in this power and experience it, the human being is able to conceive both sides of reality, unified in the power of thinking.

Truth is present when thinking becomes power, and is experienced as a flowing, unifying stream that consists of the two living sides of reality that are divided in normal consciousness - perception and understanding, the world and the I.

165

Doubt arises when the I is separated from the world, where the I searches for harmony with the world by groping about in the shady realm of abstract thinking. However, in doing this, the I constantly has to put up with insecurity, for even truths once discovered can be wrenched loose from security by doubt. This does indeed give rise to mobility, but it is a mobility of abstract appearances. It is never a fully harmonious reflection of a truly mobile power of living thinking, but a world of half truths and insecurity.

We shall now try to comprehend understanding by going into a part of Hegel's "Science of Logic", Part II. Hegel gives an impressive statement about the general, or universal, concept (*Begriff*) as the being of understanding. We find this presented in the chapter 'Subjective Logic, or the Doctrine of the Notion' (*Begriff*).

"The pure Notion [or concept, *Begriff*] is the absolutely infinite, unconditioned and free. It is here, at the outset of the discussion which has the Notion for its *content,* that we must look back once more at its genesis. *Essence* is the *outcome of being,* and the Notion, the *outcome* of essence, therefore also of being. But this becoming has the significance of a *self-repulsion,* so that it is rather the *outcome* which is the *unconditioned and original. Being,* in its transition into essence, has become an *illusory being* or a *positedness, and becoming or* transition into an *other* has become a positing; and conversely, the *positing* or reflection of essence has sublated itself and has restored itself as a being that is *not posited,* that is *original.* The Notion is the interfusion of these moments, namely, qualitative and original being is such only as a positing, only as a return-into-self, and this pure reflection-into-self is a sheer *becoming-other or determinateness* which, consequently, is no less an infinite, self-relating *determinateness.*
Thus the Notion is, in the first instance, the *absolute self-identity* that is such only as the negation of negation or as the

infinite unity of the negativity with itself. This *pure relation* of the Notion to itself, which is this relation by positing itself through the negativity, is the *universality* of the Notion.

As universality is the utterly *simple* determination, it does not seem capable of any explanation; for an explanation must concern itself with definitions and distinctions and must apply predicates to its object, and to do this to what is simple, would alter rather than explain it. But the simplicity which constitutes the very nature of the universal is such that, through absolute negativity, it contains *within itself* difference and determinateness in the highest degree. *Being* is simple as *immediate* being; for that reason it is only something *meant or intended* and we cannot say of it what it is; therefore, it is one with its other, with *non-being*. Its Notion is just this, to be a simplicity that immediately vanishes in its opposite; it is *becoming. The universal,* on the contrary, is *that simplicity* which, because it is the Notion, no less possesses *within itself the richest content.*

First, therefore, it is the simple relation to itself; it is only *within itself. Secondly,* however, this identity is *within itself* absolute *mediation,* but it is not something *mediated.* The universal that is *mediated,* namely, the *abstract* universal that is opposed to the particular and the individual, this will be discussed later when we are dealing with the specific notion. Yet even the *abstract* universal involves this, that in order to obtain it we are required to *leave out* other determinations of the concrete. These determinations, simply as such, are *negations;* equally, too, the *omitting of* them is a *negating.* So that even with the abstraction,

168

we have the negation of the negation. But this double negation is conceived of as though it were *external* to the abstraction, as though not only were the other omitted properties of the concrete distinct from the one retained, which is the content of the abstract universal, but also as though this operation of omitting the other properties and retaining the one were a process outside the properties themselves. To such an *externality* in face of that movement, the universal has not yet determined itself; it is still within itself that absolute mediation which is, precisely, the negation of the negation or absolute negativity. By virtue of this original unity it follows, in the first place, that the first negative, or the *determination,* is not a limitation for the universal which, on the contrary, *maintains itself therein* and is positively identical with itself. The categories of being were, as Notions, essentially these identities of the determinations with themselves in their limitation or otherness; but this identity was only *in itself* the Notion; it was not yet manifested. Consequently, the qualitative determination as such was lost in its other and had for its truth a determination *distinct* from itself. The universal, on the contrary, even when it posits itself in a determination, *remains* therein what it is. It is the soul [*Seele*] of the concrete which it indwells, unimpeded and equal to itself in the manifoldness and diversity of the concrete. It is not dragged into the process of becoming, but *continues* itself through that process undisturbed and possesses the power of unalterable, undying self-preservation.

But even so, it does not merely *show,* or have an *illusory being,* in its other, like the determination of reflection;

169

this, as a *correlate,* is not merely self-related but is a *positive relating* of itself to its other in which it *manifests itself;* but, in the first instance, it only *shows* in it, and this illusory being of each in the other, or their reciprocal determining, along with their self-dependence, has the form of an external act. The *universal,* on the contrary, is posited as the *essential being* of its determination, as the latter's own *positive nature.* For the determination that constitutes its negative is, in the Notion, simply and solely a *positedness;* in other words, it is, at the same time, essentially only the negative of the negative, and is only as this identity of the negative with itself, which is the universal. Thus the universal is also the *substance* of its determinations; but in such wise that what was a *contingency* for substance, is the Notion's own *self-mediation,* its own *immanent reflection.* But this mediation which, in the first instance, raises contingency *to necessity,* is the *manifested* relation; the Notion is not the abyss of formless substance, or necessity as the inner identity of things or states distinct from, and limiting, one another; on the contrary, as absolute negativity, it is the shaper and creator, and because the determination is not a limitation but is just as much utterly sublated, or posited, the illusory being is now manifestation, the manifestation *of the identical.*

The universal is therefore free power; it is itself and takes its other within its embrace, but without *doing violence* to it; on the contrary, the universal is, in its other, in peaceful communion with itself. We have called it free power, but it could also be called *free love and boundless blessedness,* for it bears itself towards its other

170

as towards *its own self;* in it, it has returned to itself.

Hegel makes an effort here – which can only be an exhausting one – to develop the concept of understanding (*Begriff des Begreifens*) as phenomenon. Thus not understanding of this or that, but understanding as achievement in thinking. While this concept of understanding falls in the 'unimaginable', the 'speechless' area of thinking which thinks itself, Hegel nevertheless attempts to put this in imaginations and words, in order to reveal to us what he has experienced. Instead of explaining the text word by word, we shall attempt to express it freely, so that the simplicity of the thought in Hegel's difficult elucidation becomes visible.

We return to the situation once again in which we are not thinking, the situation prior to the initiation of the thinking process. Because we have made a start with meditation, it becomes easier for us to persist first in a thought, but later also in powerful not-thinking. We slowly develop the ability to avert all thought associations and to know how we can remain in this thought-free void. We lern to know how to 'think not yet'. We are now thoroughly familiar with the exercise of initiating thinking, so we are able to hold it back. In this way we develop the ability to remain fully consciously in a state of not-thinking. What Hegel calls 'pure being' (*reines Sein*) thus becomes an experience for us.

In the moment we realize that we *are,* without thinking anything, we can also call this state of being (*Sein*), *nothingness.* However, as soon as we have determined that this state of being is either being or nothingness, then we have stepped back from pure being and have entered into reflection. That which reflects is an 'essence' (*Wesen*), and this essence, which I myself am, determines the 'being' - with which I was before completely at one - to be 'being' or 'nothingness'. This determination or naming makes being into appearance, or semblance, a particular memory of a state that has been experienced. This transition from a state of absorption in being (*Sein*), or nothingness (*Nichts*), into reflection is a *becoming (Werden)*. Thus can the essence (*Wesen*) also reflect upon itself, whereby it becomes aware of *itself* as a memory. It becomes an appearance itself, it sees the appearance, or facade, in that which is different from itself, because it is no longer in the present, no longer absorbed in being (*Sein*), but remembers itself as 'have been', as having reflected. Through reflection this essence *becomes* a concept (*Begriff*).

Here we are balancing, as it were, on the transition from not-thinking to thinking. We are no longer *not* thinking; we are still thinking about nothing else than about not-thinking and thinking itself. It is a 'thinking about', a reflecting on a previous experience. At this point of balance we can get to know the difference between experiencing and understanding (conceiving). If in the meantime we have the persistence to remain at this point of balance, and then to move from this point into not-thinking or into understanding the experience, then we get to know the difference between the experience which is not understood but lived through, and the experience which is no longer lived through, but understood. And we learn to understand how, in order to understand something, we have to pull

172

ourselves out of the experience constantly to allow the experience to become an appearance, a semblance that is understood. Here arises the concrete experience – and it is an extremely painful one – that all lively experience has to become mere appearance whenever we want to understand. We experience that the primal phenomenon that is the 'state' of our mind forces us to distance ourselves from the experience in order to understand it. We therefore experience our thinking as a semblance, because we first effect a division between ourselves and the experience, which we subsequently abolish by understanding. However, this has a price: *experience transforms from being into semblance, from experience into memory.*

In the chapter on philosophy I sought to point out the path from thinking as semblance (*Schein*) to thinking as being (*Sein*) by showing – and pointing out the possibility to make this one's own experience – that there is *one* point where we do not have to bring about this division in order to understand the experience. That point becomes experience that is understood and understanding that is experienced when I *as thinker initiate my thinking*, whereby it is not about thinking about this or that, but about becoming aware in the *now* of the transition from *being* that is not understood (not-thinking) to semblance/appearance that *is* understood. We do not pass over automatically into reflection, but we observe ourselves as understanding beings, we understand our cognising, as phenomenon. It is a fulcrum, a hypomochlion, a point of balance, at which we can learn to rest, undisturbed by the instability that results when we move only a little away from the fulcrum. We are then in ourselves neither quite fully in the experience nor understanding at a distance. At the fulcrum point we are completely one with ourselves as understanding beings and we experience that a world can appear at this point which can reveal itself neither in being one with the experience nor in dividing oneself through understanding. Thus, with Hegel, we can call this 'free power, free love and unlimited blessing', "for it bears itself towards [the] other as towards its own self; in it, it has returned to itself."

We thus learn in understanding ourselves to differentiate between: giving ourselves to something without understanding it, understanding something from a distance , and giving ourselves to our understanding (*Begreifen*). Through the last of these we gain the capability to understand our experience from the inside out, without distance and while maintaining our self-awareness.

From the understanding of the self-experience, we know when we understand abstractly in our cognising, and when things *understand themselves in us*.

FORM AND SUBSTANCE

When, independently from sense-perception, we construct a concept - as we have shown can be done with
mathematical thinking - we can compose this concept
because we can give *form* to it by means of the categories
which are present in our thinking. We have seen how we
construct the common concept of the circle using the
categories space, relation, and quantity. The categories
then, give the form; the formed concept is the substance.
Form and substance (matter) are in this case quite apart
from sense perception. We find the concept of the circle;
this concept is the content, the substance of our thinking.
We *come* to this substance thanks to the form, which we
have at our disposal in the categories, and which – to the
degree that we are able to observe and experience our own
thought activity ever more exactly – we learn to experience
as the primal principles that live in our mind and which
make possible the infinite variety of which our thinking is
capable. The differentiating of the primal form leads to this
infinitely differentiated thought substance.

Hegel shows us how there is a primal category, an
*un*differentiated primal form, which is the form for
constructing the concept of understanding *itself, the universal
concept*. What we find then, is an infinitely undifferentiated
primal *substance* which coincides with the primal *form*.
This becoming one, this being one, this one-being, brings
us the 'boundless blessing', for we experience neither

division nor differentiation between form and substance.

However, being human means to *summon up the courage* again and again to step out of this state of blessedness and into development, to effect division and differentiation, but without forgetting that unification was possible and always will be.

The primal category now, this undefined primal form of the concept, differentiates itself in the inner life through the forming of a specific concept, as we have shown in the case of a mathematical concept. This differentiation, which is directed outward, gives us the possibility to differentiate in the chaos of the sense perception.

We can also call substance that which comes to us through sense perception, but by this we mean the substance which approaches us from out of the world. Without the categories in our thinking, this substance would remain formless to us and undifferentiated. Because of the fact that the form principle of the categories is at work *within* observation, we cognise the multiplicity of sense perceptions; we experience ourselves cognising in a world of colour, sound, distance, time, etc.

However, in the contemporary condition of consciousness, the human being does not have the capacity to observe these different processes in cognising as a natural gift. If he seeks to gain this capacity, he must strengthen his thinking through meditation so that his thinking *itself* becomes a perceptible substance. If he manages this, then he makes the overwhelming discovery that *this* substance is the *form* that he employs as categories and that on the one hand, he directs them to sense perception, and on the other hand, directs them to the judgment that understands, that is, to the composed concept.

This form-giving substance, this substantial form, which *is* our thinking, has two faces, one of which looks to the outside, and the other to the inside. However, in our normal consciousness, instead of this one world with its faces, we experience a duality; we experience ourselves as I, over against the world.

Through our developing consciousness, we get to know the unity of both worlds – the inside and the outside world – through and through. We experience how the world of understanding is a purely spiritual inner world in which, as thinking human beings, we bring differentiated sense-perceptions into the equally richly differentiated complexes of concepts which, in their 'insight' go beyond categorised perceptions that are not grasped by a concept.

Thus we find Kant's world of the 'thing in itself' (*Ding an sich*) not 'behind' the world outside, but *inside* the unification of the outer and inner worlds through our inner comprehending spirit, which is always penetrating the outside, always forming substance, always lending substance to form. Without a strengthening of thinking through meditation there will develop an ever greater division in science between form and substance. Thinking will increasingly be experienced as semblance. The consciousness of form will be lost and will only be applied, unrecognised and unconsciously, in order to be able to absorb the immense growth of substance (factual knowledge) which arises from observation. The human being will be overwhelmed through the senses by formless substance. The human being will have to exert himself more and more in order to give form to this outer substance. The world of inner understanding, of one's giving form to substance in the conceptual world – which is the world of the 'thing in itself', but which lives *inside* us – will fade away more and more and the human being will *lose himself to the world*. A prejudice will have to be cultivated more and more to deal with this in order to create a counter-pressure against the supremacy of the world over the I. In undeveloped, abstract thinking we are in danger of losing ourselves when we observe. We encounter ourselves by maintaining ourselves in our prejudice. Through the prejudice that I have myself formed, I know that I am. Also, in forming a hypothesis we bear ourselves out into the world so as not to lose our self-consciousness. Through this, despite scientists' claims to objectivity, subjectivity is actually far more ensconced in science than one commonly thinks. Inside us there is a great resistance against letting go of this subjective activity; for then we lose ourselves.

By, as it were, continually mingling ourselves in our judgments about the world, we maintain a sort of self-awareness. Indeed, we tend to call someone a *strong* personality who exhibits a certain strong self-awareness of this kind. We like to cultivate our own judgments, our own opinions; we like discussions which are fights to distinguish who has the strongest personality. 'There are many paths,

178

everyone has his own truth'.

The path indicated in this book is not one of the cultivation of one's own opinion. It is a path on which we seek universal truth, with many sides – one has to abandon the cultivation of personal opinions, one has to clear one*self* of subjectivity by learning to live in non-personal content. In thinking which experiences itself and conceves itself one finds the clue. Here lives the I in purity itself.

When one learns to rest in this point, one can maintain oneself, experiencing purity *also* when one stands eye to eye with everything else in the world, and with other people. Instead of combining facts hastily, pressing on busily from the one to the other impression, one learns to rest in his pure self, the I, and to take in what is perceived. One finds a peaceful surrender to the world, through which the static character of that world passes over steadily into an experiencing of the creative movement which precedes the stasis and which then breaks up the stasis again.

In the common abstract thinking consciousness we always observe the world as a world of static facts, in which there is movement through the elements living in there – planetary movements, storms, ebb tide and flood, plant growth, lively animals and moving human beings being moved by emotions, etc. But in all this we never observe the *movement itself.* The world view changes continuously by going from one static state into another. We always see this in the *result*; the moving effects themselves escape us, except – as described in the chapter Philosophia – at the point where we ourselves, and no one and nothing else but we ourselves are the movement and initiate it, in our *thinking*.

A powerful peacefulness in this point, strengthened by meditative practice, awakens the perceptivity for the forces of growing and withering in nature. We observe these forces with a new sense, the sense of pure, self-experiencing thinking. With this sense we observe the world-thoughts.

Thus we have founded a whole new scientific method of cognition, which proceeds from the ancient call, "Oh Man, know yourself!", but now construed in an objective sense. It leads from this self-knowledge to knowledge of the world; it is a mode of cognition in which the unification of substance (matter) and form is continuously gained. This unification is first found in the thinking of the I as a concept, as an understanding. To this new science of the world, of everything else other than thinking, also belongs getting to know other human beings, which is realized in every new 'acquaintance', even if the 'knowledge' acquired is very slight. In this area of knowing, usually the greatest subjectivity prevails; prejudice has its greatest influence here. The statement 'What John says about Peter tells us more about John than about Peter' is a simple expression of this. We have to be very strong in our pure cognitive capacity if we want to get to know someone without 'manipulating' him as we do so. Martin Buber has written a work *Das dialogische Prinzip* (The Dialogical Principle)[21], in which he movingly witnesses two possible ways in which the human being relates to the world. He calls the 'common' relation the 'I-It' relation: the human being has a subjective-abstract view of the world; he stands *opposite* to the other, makes the other into an object, into an 'it', and considers this 'it' critically from his own standpoint. But, he writes, there is another possible relation, which he calls the 'I-You' relation: the one individual 'I' *really* meets the other individual 'You', who is not made into a thing, an 'it', but is experienced with respect in his dignity, and left in his dignity, because of which, the real power of the I begins to stream to and fro between the two. Thus originates *true* community in the spirit between one human being and another, and also the Christian words "where two or three are gathered together in my Name, there am I among them" become true, *also outside* a religious community.

In Buber's words:

"For where there is no holding back between human beings, even though it be wordless, there the dialogical word has been spoken sacramentally."[22] And: "Only the being whose otherness is accepted by my being as confronting me in his full existence bears to me the rays of eternity. Only when two say to each other, with all that they are: "You are the one" does the real essence live in between them." [23]

Now and then in everyday life each one of us has known moments of merciful unification, when this 'I and You' experience *happens* to us. The path defined here makes it possible for the human being, in pure, inner activity, *to create* this moment in the encounter with other people. The taking in of the 'You' into one's self-conscious I, without prejudice, in a spirit of wonder and understanding unleash forces in the encounter which cause you and I can to rise above ourselves. Only in this way is a social renewal possible.

181

May this declaration about the highest art which one can practise – the art of meeting, the social art – which is a fruit of the development of a true philosophia and a true science, be a prelude to the next chapter about true love.

The poet Novalis (Friedrich von Hardenberg) brings the character of the new science into expression in the following poem.[24]

When numbers and figures
Are not anymore the keys to all creatures,
When they who sing and kiss
Know more than all the deeply learned,
When the world returns once more
To a free life and its own (free) world,
When light and shadow once more
Are married to wakeful clarity,
And in fairy tales and poems
Men see the (old) true histories of the world,
Then at a single secret word will flee away
This entirely distorted existence.

Novalis – Materials for 'Heinrich von Ofterdingen'
The Berlin Papers. August 1800.

LOVE

LOVE

'How, moved thereto only by love,
He gave Himself to us entirely
And laid Himself within the earth -
Foundation stone of a city divine?'

Novalis, Spiritual Songs no. XI.

The word 'love' has many meanings. Here we want to develop a pure concept of love, love as a pure concept. If we fill our pure, powerful thinking fully with this pure concept, which becomes *deed*, we find love as power and can form it then, cleansed by spirit, in our deeds. In the chapter Philosophia we found the light with which we can enlighten our own thinking, our own light, and inflame it. We have then found pure self- consciousness.

In the chapter Science we saw how we can maintain this self-consciousness in cognising everything else in life besides thinking. We then stand with a spiritual self-consciousness in the world and can exclude all our 'own' content in this self-consciousness, in order to experience, with full devotion for the world, how this outer world speaks itself inside our self-consciousness.

We have found beauty and purity in self-conscious thinking. We found truth in cognising everything else. However, we become truly *good* people through good actions. Can we also find certainty in this area? Is there a path that we can follow, which enables us to become people who know when they do good? Can we also answer this question in such a way that the answer is not realized abstractly, but is given from direct experience?

We shall first give an extensive description of the various common meanings of the word love, in order then to find love as true human *strength* that is active in all conscious *good* deeds.

The most fundamental form of love is the desire to have something, to gain possession of it. Even if many people do not want to see this desire as love, nevertheless it *is* love. Even material greed, greed for money that becomes avariciousness, is a form of love. All greed is passion, it is fiery, it is nothing tepid or lukewarm. I desire something because I think that it is beautiful, valuable, pleasant, etc. In *that* recognition which precedes my desire, and which then comes together with my desire, lives my love for the object. That I subsequently want to make the object my possession, which one could call a selfish motive, does not detract from my love for the object.

A tragic natural law in the life of desire is now that the love for the object disappears sooner or later *because* the object has become possession. It becomes 'ordinary' to have it in your possession, the eagerness for it is gone. Thus

186

love for the *desire itself* arises, i.e. one falls in love with the passionate desire for an object, seeks satisfaction and this stirs up a new desire. The original love for the object becomes a lust to satisfy the desire for the sake of one's own self; one gets trapped more and more in the desire to feel oneself in the fire; it is no longer about the object, it is about the self.

This also holds true in a sexual relationship that is exclusively founded on the pleasure of the desire to be satisfied, and in enjoying the satisfaction. The satisfaction then is followed by the relaxation of the passionate desire; the desire passes, but in the silence of this moment the absence of desire reawakens, and the process then starts all over again. Where originally the desire was awakened by love for the beauty of the other or for the charisma of the other, or for the erotic game with the other, in sex one ultimately loses the other and experiences only oneself. Not everyone will agree with this statement. But anyone who looks at his desires honestly and without prejudice, who does not distance himself from them but really ventures to dive into them, will have to acknowledge to himself that this natural law in the life of desire constantly reasserts itself.

We find a higher, nobler form of love in the love that is based on blood relations. The love of a mother for her child, of the child for the mother, is a pure example of that. Here it is about a 'natural' love, a love from out of nature, from heredity. Here desire is not the driving power, here it is the physical, bodily relationship, the profundity of belonging together through flesh and blood, which is the driving force in love. These are literally *unrecognised* forces, which, with real effect, constantly ignite love between people. The development of this love relationship to higher forms, in accordance with the developmental stage of the child, is the foundation stone of a true education of the child. When the child grows up on this strong, steady bodily foundation of love, then love grows for the real being of the child, for the course of his life and for his ideals – however different his life-path and ideals may differ from those of his parents.

The next form of natural love, of noble love based on nature, is that love which finds its roots in the forces of a people, a nation. This is love for one's own nation – the love for fatherland or motherland - patriotism. In our time we no longer really see this patriotism come to life in a noble and natural form; today we know it mostly in its degenerated form of antipathy against other peoples or races. Nevertheless, the noble form of patriotism does exist. And who does not know the genuine emotions that are stirred while listening to one's own national anthem? Also this form of natural love – because of course it blossoms from the connection through birth and upbringing with a city or a nation – can develop itself; it can be developed into a love that crosses boundaries and which can grow into true philanthropy, into love for the world. The urge to *ignore* the real, effective forces that constitute love of country is pointless; one must want to get acquainted with them in order to be able to develop them consciously.

The following step of love shows how love becomes free of the natural connections of desire, blood and nation and takes the form that is based on experiencing one's own soul *through* the love of another. When I know I am loved by another human being, I experience myself in happiness. Another's love enlightens my own being and also makes it shine for myself. Thus the other becomes important to me; I start to love him because of his love for me. It will be clear that the driving force of this love in the beginning is not love for the other, but an experiencing of one's self, a selfish impulse. But here too, love can develop when the joy that the other has because of me, sets my own soul on fire too in enthusiasm for the other.

Thus we enter an even purer area in love if, without an external reason and totally from out of ourselves, we are capable to feel love for the beauty of the body, the truthfulness of the soul and the goodness of the spirit of the other human being. Love for the beautiful body is love that moves in the realm of the perceptible. Higher love is love for the truthfulness of the soul of the other, and even higher stands the love for the goodness that the other shows through the deeds that spring from his spirit. Thus someone whose love is altruistic, who is not looking out for experiencing himself, but feels the love that can enjoy the beauty, the truthfulness and goodness of the other, and who can find joy in that - this person can take the first step in the development of the highest love that a human being can develop. Only he who is capable of this true philanthropy can develop a pure, desire-free love for the beauty of nature. Only in nature – where there is no direct contact possible with soul and spirit, where we can not communicate through words with the organisms like we can with fellow men, can someone who has learned to experience human beauty as the expression of the soul and spirit living inside him, have love for that which expresses itself in nature: the creative world-word.

One could think that it is easier to have love for nature, than for a human being, because the human being also carries evil inside him and does evil, while one can not say this of nature. One overlooks then the fact that the human being is able to *speak* the creative world-word; he is not *mute*. He is able to make himself known to the other because he is a thinking and speaking being, because of which he is able to show himself to any other being possessed of senses. Nature shows itself in silence, making the world-word known through shapes, colours, fragrances, actions. We can not deliberate with her about what she wants to say; we have to develop a new sense in order to listen to her, as described in the chapter 'Science'.

We find in art the transition from love for the sensory to love for the transcendental, the suprasensory. Art is true art for as far as it expresses *more* than a copy of reality. If a painting shows an exact resemblance to what everyday sense perception observes, it is no art. Art is present when the artist knows how to reproduce what he has perceived in observing with his spirit. If he knows how to embody *that* in colour, sound, matter, word, or rhythm, he carries the ideal element into the sense perceptible world. Thus to 'everyday' observation that becomes visible which otherwise can only be seen with the spirit.

In our time, everything that is embodied in colour, sound etc. is called art, even if it expresses *less* than a copy of reality. If in 'art', lusts, desires etc. are expressed, we are dealing with the counterpart of true art, which is an expression of ideal beauty.

One who has love for this expression of ideas in matter has love for the beauty in art. Thus art can become a teacher to us, helping us to perceive the transcendental in the world. We need the courage then, to *dare* to see more in nature than our senses and our reason show us in the first instance. The narrow-minded man seeks in art the exact copy of sense perception. The lover of true art awakens his own artistic powers by the courage to acknowledge the transcendental aspect of true art.

Here we find the transition to love for the transcendental, the first step of which is love for the beauty of ideas.

In Plato's *Symposion* Socrates speaks of this ideal of love of beauty, quoting the wise Diotima as follows:[25]

"...he who would proceed aright in this matter should begin in youth to watch beautiful forms; and first, if he be guided by his instructor aright, to love one such form only-out of that he should create fair thoughts; and soon he will of himself perceive that the beauty of one form is akin to the beauty of another; and then if beauty of form in general is his pursuit, how foolish would he be not to recognise that the beauty in every form is and the same! And when he perceives this he will abate his violent love of the one, which he will despise and deem a small thing, and will become a lover of all beautiful forms; in the next stage he will consider that the beauty of the mind is more honourable than the beauty of the outward form. So that if a virtuous soul have but a little comeliness, he will be content to love and tend him, and will search out and bring to the birth thoughts which may improve the young, until he is compelled to contemplate and see the beauty of aspirations and laws, and to understand that the beauty of them all is of one family, and that personal beauty is a trifle; and after laws and aspirations he will go on to the sciences, that he may see their beauty, being not like a servant in love with the beauty of one youth or man or aspiration, himself a slave mean and narrow-minded, but drawing towards and contemplating the vast sea of beauty, he will create many fair and noble thoughts and notions in boundless love of wisdom; until on that shore he grows and waxes strong, and at last the vision is revealed to him of a single science, which is the science of beauty everywhere. To this I will proceed; please to give me your very best attention:

He who has been instructed thus far in the things of love, and who has learned to see the beautiful in due order and succession, when he comes toward the end will suddenly perceive a nature of wondrous beauty (and this, Socrates, is the final cause of all our former toils) - a nature which in the first place is everlasting, not growing and decaying, or waxing and waning; secondly, not fair in one point of view and foul in another, or at one time or in one relation or at one place fair, at another time or in another relation or at another place foul, as if fair to some and-foul to others, or in the likeness of a face or hands or any other part of the bodily frame, or in any form of speech or knowledge, or existing in any other being, as for example, in an animal, or in heaven or in earth, or in any other place; but beauty absolute, separate, simple, and everlasting, which without diminution and without increase, or any change, is imparted to the ever-growing and perishing beauties of all other things.

He who from these ascending under the influence of true love, begins to perceive that beauty, is not far from the end. And the true order of going, or being led by another, to the things of love, is to begin from the beauties of earth and mount upwards for the sake of that other beauty, using these as steps only, and from one going on to two, and from two to all fair forms, and from fair forms to fair practices, and from fair practices to fair notions, until from fair notions he arrives at the notion of absolute beauty, and at last knows what the essence of beauty is."

Who does not see an abstract made-up idea in this train of thought, but can experience a living reality in it, finds the description of the highest experience that Philosophia can give – Philosophia interpreted here as indispensable love for beauty, for the purity of sense-free thinking, for wisdom. The experience of the I, creating in beauty, the I that has freed itself of connections to the senses, connections to the body and which has purified itself that it can create and experience in this pure, sense-free thinking.

In the twelfth book Lambda of his Metaphysics (chapter 7),

Aristotle speaks in the same vein, in relation to the 'best':[26]

"And thinking in itself deals with that which is best in itself, and that which is thinking in the fullest sense with that which is best in the fullest sense. The thinking spirit thinks itself because it shares the nature of the object of thought; for it becomes an object of thought in coming into contact with the thought, so that the thinking spirit and the object of thought are the same. For that which is capable of receiving the object of thought, i.e. the essence, is the thinking spirit. And he realises it by making it his own. Therefore the possession rather than the receptivity is the divine element which the thinking spirit seems to contain, and the act of contemplation is what is most pleasant and best. If, then, God is always in that good state in which we sometimes are, this compels our wonder; and if in a better this compels it yet more.

And life also is in God; for the realisation of the thinking spirit is life, and God is that actuality; and God's self-dependent actuality is life most good and eternal. We say therefore that God is a living being, eternal, most good, so that life and duration continuous and eternal being belong to God; for this is God."

Here Aristotle describes how, when it directs itself to what is 'the best', the thinking spirit experiences itself as thinking in itself. It experiences then the congruence of thinking in itself with the thinker, the I, the thought, and the metamorphosis of the I in the thoughts.

If thinking directs itself to the best, which is the I, then the I metamorphoses itself the best, in pure thoughts, in

194

beauty. The union of the I, the best, with its creation, with thought, with beauty, brings truth and the conquest of doubt.

As beauty knows herself to be connected to her origin, the best, in this experience religion (literally, reuniting) is realized in the most literal sense.

What is thought here finds its origin again in the thinker, and he knows that his own origins are in the best. The fiery power of will that is directed to the good brings warmth and light in thinking itself and reveals there the reuniting of the thinker with his thoughts. Thus philosophy becomes religion.

We may fill our thinking with religious *content*, yet God remains for us a mental representation, and this mental representation is always subject to doubt. Whoever thinks that true faith is only to be found in the life of mental representations, or in the imagined life of feeling and will, gives himself over to a misunderstanding which works destructively on his faith.

We should not think that that individual is arrogant or conceited who strives hard to find the best inside himself which he conceives to be the likeness of God. He is not suffering from the delusion that he is equal to God; he knows himself to be created in God's likeness when he represents the best that he can be. Conceit is present, rather, where the human being thinks he was born 'complete', where he just accepts himself as he is and in false humility satisfies himself with his human subjective imaginations of God.

'Intellect can certainly shape,
But the dead can not ensoul.
Everything living springs only
From what is alive.'

These poetic words of *Goethe* sharply express the limitation of the human intellect, the life of mental representations. Setting boundaries to human knowledge and the proclaiming faith as a duty to lie outside these boundaries is no humility but a conceit. The *only thing* that we have left in our western life as a real divine force, is *not* the religious content of our life of mental representations, but what we as human beings will to make of ourselves in God's likeness.

This too can be illustrated with a poem by Goethe:[27]

THE GODLIKE

'Noble be man,
Helpful and good!
For that alone
Distinguisheth him
From all the beings
Unto us known.

Hail to the beings,
Unknown and glorious,
Whom we forebode!
From his example
Learn we to know them!

For unfeeling
Nature is ever:
On bad and on good
The sun alike shineth;
And on the wicked,

As on the best,
The moon and stars gleam.

Tempest and torrent,
Thunder and hail,
Roar on their path,
Seizing the while,
As they haste onward,
One after another.

Even so, fortune
Gropes 'mid the throng--
Innocent boyhood's
Curly head seizing,--
Seizing the hoary
Head of the sinner.

After laws mighty,
Brazen, eternal,
Must all we mortals
Finish the circuit
Of our existence.

Man, and man only
Can do the impossible;
He 'tis distinguisheth,
Chooseth and judgeth;
He to the moment
Endurance can lend.

He and he only
The good can reward,
The bad can he punish,
Can heal and can save;
All that wanders and strays
Can usefully blend.

And we pay homage
To the immortals
As though they were men,
And did in the great,
What the best, in the small,

Does or might do.

Be the man that is noble,
Both helpful and good.
Unweariedly forming
The right and the useful,
A type of those beings
Our mind hath foreshadow'd!

1782.

It is not about forming images about the good God, as if he were far away from us, unreachable; it is about the divine *inside us*, what we can realize by our good, noble, helpful deeds, so we get to know God *in our deeds* as He who accomplishes in great measure what we do in small measure or seek to do if only we proceed from what is 'best' in us.

St. Thomas Aquinas spoke in the same way about the relationship between the inner life of human being with the divine. We quote from: his Commentary on the Gospel of St John (I, 1-11).[28]

"Secondly, from what has been said, we are able to understand that a word is always something that proceeds from the spirit in an living intellect existing in act; and furthermore, that a word is always a notion (ratio) and image of the thing understood. So if the thinker and the thought are the same, then the word is a notion and an image of the spirit from which it proceeds. On the other hand, if the thinker is other than the thought, then the word is not an image and notion of the thinker but of the thing understood, as the mental representation which one has of a stone is an image of only the stone. But when the spirit thinks itself, its word is an image and notion of the spirit. And so Augustine (On the Trinity IX, 5) sees an image of the Trinity in the Soul insofar as the mind thinks itself, but not insofar as it thinks other things. It is clear then that it is necessary to presume that the word is in all spiritual beings, for the understanding of thinking shows us that the spirit forms something by thinking: what is formed is called Word. And so we must presume the word in all thinking beings."

What we find in Goethe's poem "The Godlike" in artistic form, we find in this text from St. Thomas Aquinas expressed in the form of logical thinking.

We do not find the origin of the highest love, the love for God, outside of us, but *in* us, there where we are created in God's image and where we may proceed with this creation directly, in freedom: in the activity of thinking in which our I lives creatively as will. No self-love is awakened in this way; what awakens is the self, the I, *as* love, as the best desire (the self as will) which longs for union with the most beautiful (pure thought) and finds in *this* union the highest truth in a continuously renewing creativity. With this we have not reached a goal; rather, we have taken the first step on a developmental path to perfection, a path with an eternal perspective.

And when we are more and more capable of getting to know the world in this awakened love then, we expand our inner pure thinking, with outer beauty, with *the cosmos*, with cosmic thoughts, with world thoughts.

Thus we also find the concept of evil, which we get to know as the forces both outside us and inside us which want to obstruct us from realizing our development. We no longer see evil as an abstract power with which we have nothing to do, or which seduces us without our knowledge. We get to know evil as an illicit development: either as a brake on our development towards the good, the true and the beautiful because we lose the courage to go on with this development in the face of all our imperfection, failures and all the resistance, or we get to know evil as the illicit acceleration of the development, whereby we surrender our *freedom* to this development: we *are* developed, instead of developing ourselves. We learn how our development is only rightful if it blossoms in full consensus with the environment, and when we ourselves cope with certainty with regard to morality – the good – in our intentions ourselves. It is not the environment that should dictate to us how we have to do the right thing; we ourselves do the good because we *want* to do it; we act in full responsibility, because we know the purity of our motives and feel the truth of them.

Thus we develop the new faith. This faith is not a consequence of weakness in the thinking process, nor is it a setting of limits to knowledge. The new faith is trust in cognition itself as a boundary crossing activity. The *experience of crossing* boundaries makes this into a faith that one is sure of, because it is not a faith in mental representations and imaginations, but an *event* which is as concrete as the experiences of life, and which we have accomplished ourselves as *the free deed of the I*: it is the first event that happens to us *because* we accomplish it ourselves. It is a destiny we ourselves wanted. But we can only accomplish this deed of the I if we kindle it in love for pure thinking.

The force which comes into life through this and which is a thinking force that we actually experience, a kindling of thinking in love, experienced in full, alert consciousness, can then as thinking love, as loving thinking, as faith in love, as love in faith, be traced back to the will to the good, as this develops in our deeds for the outer world. And when this thinking force kindled in love provides the motives for our deeds, when this love can be maintained in the consciousness of our deeds, then we develop *true virtue*, which is a love for the deed that is borne by our certainty about the origin of our motives, out of our good will, our best, our love. The reader who still wishes to follow me here can experience with me that this love springs from the spirit and is led into the limbs which carry out what are then fully conscious deeds.

Through this, our will receives a new quality that is alive and free. A concept comes into being that has been but a *word* up to this point, and which has to be known deep down in the will in order to bring it to life: it is hope, hope as a driving force in our good, loving, convincing will that is given for the world.

Will in thinking brings us faith.
The knowledge of the will awakens hope.
The wakening force is always love.

'How, moved thereto only by love,
He gave Himself to us entirely
And laid Himself within the earth -
Foundation stone of a city divine.'

CONTEMPLATION

ABSTRACT AND LIVING THINKING

That which I wanted to express in this work has now been said.

However, every pure thinking activity always calls for contemplation, even when one is fully aware in this thinking activity and its resulting content. After all, when we want to give shape in the spirit to an insight we always have to step out of this insight – which is at the same time an overview – into the thinking process, into the *line* of thought. We thereby withdraw from the insight and overview and engage in the effort of carrying over that which was present at *one* point of thought. We have to search for many words to make the insight visible from different sides and render it comprehensible. And with the withdrawal from this point of insight, we directly experience the inadequacy of our words and the patchy character of our thinking, because of which the description of what was seen at the point of insight will always be imperfect. Accordingly, this work can not end here, and a reflection is necessary – which will also be incomplete – on the encounter of the reasoning developed here with already existing views.

In the previous chapters a developmental path of thinking has been described, on which, after one has found oneself as thinker, *which is the first step* - one experiences pure will in this thinking. One finds the *will* as a point coincident with one's I, as an undefined force, which will reveal itself through deeds in the future. The first differentiation that one finds in this I as will is the willing thinker, who differentiates himself in actively formed thoughts. The willing I silently confronts the world, silent in thinking, not without participating in it, but silently in full active attention, differentiating itself in true thoughts *in* everything else in life. The I is being thought, willing by everything else. In the I, actively silent in full devotion, the world thinks itself. This entering of the world-thoughts in the attentive, willing I is pure love, which encourages deeds that are in full agreement with the truth of one's own I *and* the truth in the world.

The reader who is familiar with the thinkers of past centuries, with the history of philosophy, shall possibly object that modern philosophy has left this reasoning far behind. Nietzsche, for example, proved how philosophy had come to an end, by reducing thinking and feeling to just reflections on a surface above a much greater depth, that of organic life. A philosophy such as the one in this book, which finds the starting-point in thinking itself, seems totally in contradiction with this and may seem to constitute a relapse in philosophy, an anachronism.

Nevertheless, with this philosophy the opposite is intended. The writer could prove how a human being like Nietzsche *executes* thinking and feeling, puts them to death, how he struggles with *his* despair about abstract thinking, how he has experienced a dragon of concepts in this and longs for a human being who can overcome this abstraction, this narrow minded man, in order to become a superman. It is actually in perceiving the will in thinking, perceiving the I as thinker, that Nietzsche could have found the way to mediate with the organic world. He would not have experienced himself any longer as forced to go *under the surface of thinking*, he would have been able to experience in thinking itself the downfall of abstraction, which would then have become an ascension, because the discovery of the will in thinking *is* the victory over abstraction. At the same time, he would have found the transition, the bridge, for a conscious entry into the organic, into his own body. This new thinking is no confined conceptual schema, no "languid but sinister, active factory of concepts and words" (Nietzsche), but a differentiated, intentional play of forces experienced as tangible reality, fully conscious, with self-consciousness fully maintained.

This thinking takes no different path from that of the instincts, but becomes the instrument for the purification of the basic instincts in the development of the highest human instinct, the love for wisdom, the desire for wisdom, philosophy. This thinking does not turn away from the body and from life, but experiences itself as a becoming aware of vitality, coming from the same source as the vitality of the organic realm and capable of seeing through this organic realm in all its effects. Thus there could have been written a complete work, a dialogue with the thoughts of philosophers like Nietzsche, Heidegger, and Habermas. This would make this present book much clearer. The short discussions of the ideas of Hegel, Heidegger, Krishnamurti and Steiner may serve as an example of that.

Philosophy has come to a boundary and wants to go

beyond itself. It serves as a warning to humanity, which has come to a border where every human being wants to go beyond himself. At this boundary philosophy can keep thinking on in the old pattern, imagining that it is modern, but in reality puffing itself up with variations on old themes.

Philosophy must go beyond itself by not *wanting* to be a reflective science any longer, but a powerful desire, a fervent desire to break through the abstract life of mental representations, to find the fire of reality in thinking. Thinking is not an obstinate conceptual apparatus, nor a word factory but a living organism, that can only know its origin and union with the organic if it has *first recognised as its prime object* the lively flame of the spiritual will, the will that is willing to think, due to which, thinking does not experience a downfall but a resurrection. The human being does not grow together with his body – if he did, his soul and his consciousness would have to die together with his physical death – he grows together with his *I*, with his spirit; thus he can live free in his body, investigate it from within and be happy with it.

Making this activity visible has been the aim of this book. It has not been about achieving any perfect result, but about the work that is needed in order to achieve an ever better result.

Questioning everything, letting nothing congeal in answers - that is a real awakened lively philosophy. Abstract thinking can be 'completed', willed thinking never is. The new thinking always points to a future that is not yet formed.

DOUBT AND CERTAINTY

In this work I have wanted to present a path along which we can overcome the phenomenon of doubt. It would be a completely wrong conclusion if one were to think that, having read and comprehended this book, one would never have to doubt again from this point on, that one would be sure of *everything*. It is not doubt in this or that which is overcome on this path, but doubting in knowledge itself, doubt about the possibility that one can know something with certainty. From the point where I have found myself as thinker *I have found the certainty that it is possible to be certain in one's knowing* - as a pure phenomenon. I know *that* I can be certain, and also *how* I can be certain, or which inner position I have to take up in order to know whether I am certain or not. This judgment: 'I am certain of my knowing', does not come about through reflection; it is a knowing which arises with knowing itself. In other words: If *my knowing is willed* from the point where I am totally aware of my self as thinker, I know exactly at the same time how certain my knowing is, and from where that point passes into speculative thinking. At that moment I leave the union of myself with my thought life, with my will, and enter the realm of mental representations. I enter the world of my imaginations, which are images of myself and the world, in which I, as thinker, am not present any longer, but in which I constantly move as a reflector between myself and the world. We are always in this position in our thinking as long as we have not found ourselves as thinkers, as reality. Here, where - unaware of ourselves – we are always coated in mental images, we are not even sure that our I is imagining anything, neither are we sure of the inner nature of *what* it is we are imagining. We are not even sure of the meaning of the imagining itself. "The world is my mental image". Even my self is an imagination. Life is a dream of mental images; nowhere do we find a passage to reality. Only when we *want* to find ourselves, as a *force*, and not as an imagined will, but as a reality that we initiate in our thinking, thus as a *doing*, do we find the first non-imagined experience in this thinking doing, which *nevertheless* comes into being in thinking. It is a waking up from a dream of mental images. This can not be understood by more mental images; it must be *done* and only then it can be criticized by the reviewer of the reasoning presented here. With pleasure, I quote in this connection Hegel in his preface to his 'Phenomenology of Spirit':[29]

"For the real subject-matter is not exhausted in its *purpose*, but in *working the matter out*; nor is *the mere result attained the concrete whole* itself, but the result along with the process of arriving at it. The purpose of itself is a lifeless universal, just as the general drift is a mere activity in a certain direction, which is still without its concrete realization; and the naked result is the corpse of the system which has left its guiding tendency behind it. Similarly, the distinctive *difference* of anything is rather the *boundary*, the limit, of the subject; it is found at that point where the subject-matter stops, or it is what this subject-matter is *not*. To trouble oneself in this fashion with the purpose and results, and again with the differences, the positions taken up and judgments passed by one thinker and another, is therefore an easier task than perhaps it seems. For instead of laying hold of the matter in hand, a procedure of that kind is all the while away from the subject altogether. Instead of dwelling within it and becoming absorbed by it, knowledge of that sort is always grasping at something else; such knowledge, instead keeping to the subject-matter and giving itself up to it, never gets away from itself. *The easiest thing of all is to pass judgments on what has a solid substantial content; it is more difficult to grasp it, and most of all difficult to do both together and produce the systematic exposition of it*[**]*."*

We would be able to characterize the philosophy which is developed in this book as a radicalization of thinking as the only phenomenon which can be thought directly without the intervention of mental representation, for it springs directly, radically, from the I, but also in the I. To employ Heidegger's choice of words: here, in thinking about thinking, initiated by the I, we find access to the question of being. In thinking which is *done* with consciousness of the I, we find an entity that exists without a forgetfulness of being. When we imagine something, we *imagine* an entity, and forget *the being* of this entity. When we think of our I as 'unimaginable', we do not only grasp an entity in our thinking, but *we ourselves are thinking itself.* An entity of being (thought), and being (the I) are completely at one here. An entity of being (*Seiendes*) *can* be without forgetfulness of being (*Sein*). We find being in the "I am".

** Emphasis - MM

We find in this "I am" the being of all entities of being (*Seiendes*) in the rest of life. We find a being, not a static one, but a being in permanent movement, in development.

THE WILLPOWER AS A BRIDGE OVER THE ABYSS

We have been introduced to doubt as the 'lacuna' between the I and thought. This lacuna develops between the I and its metamorphosis, thought, because the human being does not in full consciousness 'drive' his thought life with his will. The thought life runs on automatically, partly associative, partly with a precise understanding, but always with a loss of I-ness. With that, I lose the responsibility for my thought life on the one hand; it runs on without me, it 'is not my fault, what I think'. On the other hand, I have lost my faith in thinking, for it is a whimsical reflection in mental images of reality. What is this reality as I represent it to myself in images?

Becoming aware of the I, as willed thinking, builds a bridge over this lacuna, this gap. I learn exactly where my thinking gives certainty and where it does not. If I and thought are one there is no lacuna, no gap. From here on, my I is no longer a mental representation, but a living concept, a living reality. And I realize that in this point, although it is no more than a point, lives the possibility to enable this living reality to spread out from this point that I experience to the rest of the world. But at the same time, the notion grows that it is really about a *point* and that I have to have the courage always to leave this point again and again in order to gain experience, in which I shall always have to dare to surrender myself to the possibility of error. The only security that remains to me then is that *I*

213

know I am sure that I have left the point of being sure.

Here one has to be braced for error. Just by getting to know certainty as a human possibility, the opposite pole of the necessity of error is experienced. What I have described in the chapter Philosophia as primal fear, the fear of having to transform oneself by moving from non-thinking to thinking, spreads itself here over the whole field of cognition as fear of failure, or error.

The I initiates thinking and with that, creates the first living thought, namely itself. In order to find the way from this point of the I to a circumferential movement of this I, *I must dare to go into the darkness of error*, in order to find, over and over again, the point of light of the I as thinker in the darkness, in order to find the union of this point of light with the light of the world. One has to have the courage to venture out in thinking, to try again over and over, to be mistaken all over again. But one has the consolation of *being aware of the possibility to be mistaken*. The absolute experience of the union of the I and the thought points up the contrast with the division of the self and the thought and thus becomes the guiding light to the truth.

We can therefore understand Nietzsche's statement in the positive sense (quote found in *Nietzsche, a Fighter against his Time* by R. Steiner):[30]

"...we are fundamentally inclined to maintain that the falsest opinions (to which the synthetic judgments a priori belong), are the most indispensable to us, that without a recognition of logical fictions, without a comparison of reality with the purely imgagined world of the absolute and immutable, without a constant counterfeiting of the world by means of numbers, man could not live — that the renunciation of false opinions would be a renunciation of life, a negation of life."

FEELING

Contemplation on the line of thought followed thus far now leads to the acknowledgement that in this book willing and thinking want to do justice to themselves as conscious activity. Feeling, however, as an independent quality, is left out of consideration. In the twentieth century, a great deal of attention has been given to the meaning of feeling, either as activity, or as mental state. Is there, in the same way that we have found thinking and willing, also a possibility to grasp feeling, without leaving the path of certainty in our research, that is to say, without taking refuge in mental representations or hypotheses?

If we point to feeling, we are confronted with the difficulty that we start to think 'about' feeling, in mental representations. From this consideration, all ideas about feeling, affection, desire, disturbance, mood, etc. have originated. We are loaded with this historical pile of ideas about feeling; they prevent us from coming to a true philosophical - or better said in this context - psychological understanding of feeling.

Thus we do not want to develop a new theory about feeling, we want to seek for it in its concrete reality, so that we can explain it directly without the use of mental representations. Feeling does not remain a 'thing in itself' but is taken up in the 'unimaginable' realm of the I. Thus we have already approached love, and with that, observed an area of feeling such as lives in the outstreaming force of living thinking in the deed, as thinking in the will. We are only able to carry living thinking into the will if we have first developed thinking to where it becomes a force we can experience. It is precisely this experience of willing thinking, the I-experience, which begins as *sensation* in one's consciousness, as a self-awakened lively sensation. Willed thinking is thus experienced, it is *felt*. As long as one only imagines the will in thinking, it is not experienced. Feeling is necessary in order to become aware of this will-power as a thinking force and to *experience* it. A mental representation or image is not felt, it is at most observed with an inner gaze. The reality of thinking is felt as *a power*.

Mental representations are always reflections, either of everything else, or of thinking itself.

The sensation of thinking as a power initiated by the I is, as it were, like going under the reflecting surface of mental representations *into* the underlying power.

This experiencing of the thinking force as inner activity makes us conscious of feeling as a positive quality, which one could call 'bliss'. One finds, because one is moving in a pure willing, pure thinking, at the same time the pure thinking of feeling, which is a pure feeling. Thus one finds feeling as a pure concept, as a concretely perceived concept which is feeling at the same time. One finds in the perception of thinking as powerful will the *perception* itself, a positive feeling: happiness, desire, joy. One feels how one is open to everything actively, full of expectation. Earlier, I described this experience as follows: questioning everything, letting nothing rigidify into answers, that is awakened philosophy. In this pure feeling one finds the

217

primal phenomenon for all positive feelings in daily life.

This positive feeling in daily life shows itself in various ways in which the character of will prevails, such as in joy, but also in pride and honour. In pure feeling there is no difference between subjective and objective: here higher and lower coalesce.

In daily life, by contrast, all feelings often go on a subjective spree, such as pride, for example. This feeling is soaked with a powerful will, but with self-will.

When, fully aware in our thinking and feeling, we can *stand* in our I, we gain full power over ourselves, we can calm the will activity, and we know too that it is we ourselves who create this calm. The I metamorphoses itself from activity in thinking into a peaceful illumination of the activity. This peaceful overview permeates the will and brings peace. The storm of activity is calmed. The developed activity of the I corresponds in daily life to *self-control*. The feeling of balance that proceeds from this self-control also manifests itself in many ways in life, for example, in devotion, humility, and gratitude.

We approach the phenomenon of negative feeling when we realise which inner condition we are in when we do not calm our will activity *ourselves*, but when this will activity is *silenced* by a factor outside ourselves. Our will is paralysed, and we become aware of this in negative feeling. To perceive this negative feeling in pure thinking is not easy, because in this condition the activity of the I is silent, the power of thinking floats away, and we return to the reflecting world of mental representations. We then have no hold on feeling anymore other than via imaginations. If we have learned through practice to become aware of our perceiving, we can *feel* in this how the power of thinking slips away from us, and we recognise the being of aversion, of antipathy. We know this being too from daily life, as a fundamental feeling of being bound, as unfreedom. The experience in which the will is forced back the most is that of *fear*. All grief and suffering, is directly related to the experience of the loss of power, caused by something outside ourselves. These negative feelings too differentiate themselves. In fear, the ground of the I is forcibly removed. In shame this is also the case, but there the I is forced to look on as a mere witness: shame is bottomless, but the I stands around it as a witnessing conscience.

I find the perfection of feeling, love, when I will in full, aware activity, without seeking my own interest, in full, active devotion to what I am doing, either in the world, or in my thinking. If I succeed in carrying peaceful attention into this devotion, filling it with that, I become aware of the being of love, the perfect feeling.

When the will is forcibly removed, this brings suffering and passivity. But the I is always present, even when it does not engage consciously. The endurance of suffering, learning to *want* to endure suffering brings with it a powerful strengthening, which can become so strong that this will reveals itself as power in thinking. Thus opens the possibility of finding the happiness of freedom in the suffering of unfreedom.

"The easiest thing of all is to pass judgments on what has a solid substantial content; it is more difficult to grasp it, and most of all difficult to do both together and produce the systematic exposition of it."

EPILOGUE

GNOTHI SEAUTON! [***]

> Great are the senses;
> The intellect is yet greater,
> Above it ranges reason,
> But over them all stands the spirit.

Bhagavad Gita.

In this book philosophy has been approached very differently from the usual manner. We have acknowledged it as an academic science, but we have also seen that it is a *step* on the path of development that the human being must take. In this sense, no human being would want to escape from philosophy. The human being at this time has an ever growing need of reflection, of contemplation on what he has done, felt and thought. He is not only interested in life, but also in *how* life is being lived, *how* the human being stands in life. The cliché: 'What am I doing exactly?' is an expression of this. Whoever asks himself this question, even if only half-consciously, is showing the desire for reflection, the will to be a philosopher.

Furthermore, we have sought to find a totally different entrance to philosophy than is common in current philosophical science. The starting point of the philosophy

---

[***] Know Yourself!

in this book is the aphorism of Apollo at the sanctuary in Delphi: *Gnothi Seauton*, know yourself!

But here now in this very starting point lies the source of possible misunderstandings, which is put into words very clearly by Goethe (Bedeutende Fördernis, 1823):

"...the significantly sounding challenge "know thyself" always appeared suspicious to me, like a trick by a band of conspiring priests who confuse men with unattainable goals and who would distract them from outer activity into an inwardness of false contemplation. Man only knows himself insofar as he knows the world, of which he only becomes aware in himself, just as he only becomes aware of himself in the world. Every new object, well observed, opens up a new organ in us. Or: "My friend, I have done the right thing, I have never thought about thinking.""

It is a justified fear in seeking to know oneself that one will lose oneself in subjectivity. There appears to be no correcting authority in the I, as there is in the outer world, which corrects wrong ideas about the inner life, such as scientific experiments that can correct possible mistakes in hypotheses about the outer world. Hypotheses about the inner life never gain solid ground under their feet, as long as they are obtained exclusively by brooding in oneself. This is why one thinks that the attempt to gain self-knowledge is inferior to the methods of natural science. This is indeed completely correct as long as one lines oneself up *opposite* oneself in self-knowledge in the same way as one confronts the other in knowledge of anything else in life. Then, with regard to the world, one finds nothing else in the self but memories, feelings, thoughts, wishes etc.

Goethe himself gives the solution elsewhere: [31]

'How can one get to know oneself? Never through one's thoughts, but rather through one's actions.'

We have found an area in our I where 'thoughts' and 'actions' fully correspond. We have found this area through thinking and we find the path described in the sentences from the Bhagavad Gita cited above in the caption.

First of all, we renounce what our senses give us: we turn our gaze inwards, withdrawing our attention from the senses and directing it to our thought world. In that thought world we apply a further degree of concentration: we silence our associative thoughts and form a concept with our mind; we take action in thought. Our mental activity is an inner act, which we observe at the same time, *because* our mind is *active*. The line of thought line does not roll on automatically, after which we observe it, but we *will* to *think* the concept, and accordingly, perception and action coalesce. In order to accomplish this coalescence, usually profound and long-term practice, soul-training, is required. Now we are very fond of physical training nowadays, but we recoil from soul-training: we are of the opinion that it should be plain sailing, we want to be able to surrender ourselves in this area. But *to what* are we surrendering then? This is a question which cannot be answered if we want to remain passive in our inner life.

225

The soul-training described leads to a point where one can fully surrender, but then one is fully aware of oneself and of 'that' to which one surrenders.

When knowing becomes doing, one has developed reason. But, even if one lives inside oneself, united with oneself in one's reason, one still has in oneself a sense content – the thought concept – which derives from the world.

The knowing will activity practised again and again, the willed knowing, leads to the moment when one becomes aware of this soul-activity as living *process*. One experiences the tingling, bubbling, whirling activity of thinking. The content fades, the process becomes observable. The last reminiscences of the world disappear, and one is then thinking in a pure spiritual, literally transcendental, world: "over them all stands the spirit".

One experiences how one is thinking supra-personally, supra-subjectively, but also supra-objectively in this pure spiritual world of living thinking activity. One has lifted oneself above the contradistinction of subject-object; one is living in a world that unites both.

'Here you should know that the masters are speaking, that there are two kinds of man in each man: the one is the outer man, the man of the senses; man is served by five senses and yet he works through the power of the soul. The other man is the inner man, this is the inner nature of man. Now you should know that every man who loves God uses no more of the soul forces of the outer man than the five senses require; and the inner nature turns not to the five senses except insofar as it is the sage and

226

leader of the five senses and it protects them so that they do not yield to their striving towards animality.'

Meister Eckhart

BEHIND THE MASK OF DOUBT

When the heart lives in despair,
The soul is in hell.
It is both ugly and lovely
When the spirit of the man of courage
Is mixed, of contrasting colours
Pied like a magpie.

Parzival - Wolfram von Eschenbach.[32]

One who has found the world of the moving, living, whirling thinking in himself, has overcome the primal phenomenon of doubt which is the result of abstract thinking. We have already pointed out that the human being is not forever saved from the actuality of doubt. One knows doubt through and through, and because of that, one knows what it means to 'be sure' and one knows that this is not conclusive in nature, but that is just the beginning of a whole new path of knowledge, whereby one has to be always fully aware and must develop full presence of mind. But an apparently new, previously unknown insecurity appears, an insecurity that seems to permeate our whole being far more strongly than doubt in knowing.

We have learned to experience ourselves in powerful, vigorous thinking and we have also learned to absorb impressions from the sensory world *in* this thinking activity: they express themselves in us as world-thoughts.

We are sure that it is the world itself that is expressing itself in our thinking. But when we return to ourselves, when we close our senses and enter again the path to self knowledge, when we live in our thinking, we live in a moving, living spiritual world. Yet we experience this world as created and sustained by our own thinking activity. We live in our own spiritual world of supra-subjective, supra-objective human wisdom.

As philosophers we strive for a world of divine wisdom, we feel love for Sophia, for the revelation of divine wisdom. It may be that we have not experienced it directly through philosophy, for not every philosopher sees a religious task in his work. As seriously, however, as we take philosophy here, every philosopher is, strictly speaking, searching for divine wisdom, or at least searching for wisdom from the spirit, as distinct from the natural scientist, who searches for knowledge of external nature. It is in this literal sense that we want to regard philo-sophy, as love for Sophia, as love for the divine wisdom.

What we have now found is human spiritual wisdom, our own spiritual world of thinking. The taking in of the world-thoughts into this spiritual world of ours extends our horizons beyond ourselves; but even if we are not then thinking ourselves, we always experience our own thinking activity as the medium through which we are acting, and when we have returned to our own transcendental, thinking world we find *nothing but ourselves*, nothing but our own power.

A whole new insecurity now appears inside us, a doubt that does not disappear in our knowing, a doubt that seems to bring no benefit with it, a doubt that challenges our whole existence in thinking: doubt in the existence of a divine-spiritual world. *I* exist, even when I close down the functioning of my senses. But does a divine-spiritual world exist outside this thinking world which I am and that can fill itself with world-thoughts? This is the loneliness of despair. Everything is thought, and thought is what *I am.* I live in a whirling, bubbling stream; this is what I am. I have found myself by *wanting to think myself.* But shall I ever find something other than myself?

This is not doubt in thinking, this is doubt in the heart.

"When the heart lives in despair,
The soul is in hell."

QUESTIONING AS VIRTUE

You will bear for ever, most worthily,
The blessed crown of healing
And there will be fulfilled for you
At the highest level a-plenty
What you on earth have wished for
And no-one, be he e'er so mighty
Shall live so glorious a life as you –
If you will only ask the question!

Parzival – Wolfram von Eschenbach.

We have found the first question, the question with which philosophy begins. The answer to that question we have not found in abstract thinking, not dubious anymore, but as an inevitable *fact*, founded on experience in internal, supra-subjective and supra-objective thinking. This has given philosophy a solid foundation.

The answer is the becoming aware of the I as the initiator of thinking. This I lives in a source of power, out of which thinking streams forth as the metamorphosis of the I. But with this ultimate answer we live in a world in which we seem to be grasping thin air. We can develop our will in thinking to the utmost, we can *want* thinking completely and we do get to know it through and through. But we have no content that we could think in our inner activity that is averted from the senses, apart from ourselves. Everything we think, there *we* are again.

Only a total inner change can release us from loneliness. The human being lives in his active thinking in the answer. The self-awakened thinking is the answer through and through, it is the *primal-answer*. Having arrived at this point, we must now silence this answer, reform it into the *primal-question*, into questioning itself.

The living thinking what we *are* must turn into a living question, a complete holding back. Thus our I turns into a questioning, not a questioning about this or that, but *the* question as the expression of yearning. In the words of Novalis: "The most beautiful gift which has been offered to man is the yearning of his soul".

The achievement of this state of mind that becomes a solid event in living thinking – the whole soul becomes a yearning question in patient expectation – is the fulfilment of philosophy: the human being is wholly love for Sophia. Not only is there not a single thought in the soul any longer, there is also no longer a single answer; the whole soul, in full awareness, is but a questioning yearning.

Thus the human being kneels, not with the body in the pew, but with his now powerful I in his silent soul and *becomes prayer.*

'To the eternal wisdom of God,
To the mirror without stain,
Which the cherubim and all
Blessed spirits with eternal
Wonder gaze upon,

To the light which enlightens
All men who come into the world,
To the inexhaustible fountain
And the primal spring of all
Wisdom,
Ascribe and direct
Once more to these
This small droplet,
Mercifully drawn from their great ocean.
A being with ceaseless longing
To look upon you,
The ever dying
Johannes Angelus'

Angelus Silesius, "The Cherubinic Wanderer"[33]

THE PHILOSOPHER IN WONDER

> When he experiences
> himself now in the being
> that is thinking in him,
> so that he rises from mere
> thinking to spiritual
> experience, then from
> this experience he gains
> an inner, pure spiritual
> power of imagination.
>
> *R. Steiner: The Riddle of Man* [34]

Which inner activity must we develop in order to change our thinking - which we have brought to life in full devotion, and which has thus become the answer to the question of philosophy - into a living question for God? How must we turn our will totally around so that it can change from answer into question? For our will *goes out of us* and develops itself in thinking, which becomes *perception*. How can we manage to totally change the direction of our will, so that we can open ourselves up to 'Thy will be done', without sinking back into a passivity that is not conscious of the I?

When we gradually learn to *experience* the living stream of thinking, the will power that proceeds from us is slowly turned into an organ that receives the pure spiritual world *outside our I*. The less our own will unfolds itself in thinking, the more it is absorbed in the experience: *It thinks within me.* Experiencing one's own spirit widens itself to experiencing the spiritual world, which does *not* express itself in the stream of thinking, but in the *experiencing* of this stream of thinking.

The stream of thinking that proceeds from us grasps in a spiritual nothingness. Experiencing the stream, the experiencing of the being that thinks in us, makes the stream turn round *to us*. In the language of mysticism:

"I must be Mary,
And give birth to God out of myself,
If He is to bless me eternally".

Angelus Silesius, The Spiritual Mary, Cherubinic Wanderer [35]

PHILOSOPHY OR ANTHROPOSOPHY

Uplifted is the stone –
And all mankind is risen –
We all remain thine own.
And vanished is our prison.
All troubles flee away
Thy golden bowl before,
For Earth and Life give way
At the last and final supper.

Novalis, Hymns to the Night [36]

We do not live alone, we live in a community with our fellow man, we live in the surrounding nature. As philosophers in a state of wonder we lead a secret inner life amidst the surrounding world of human beings and nature.

We find in "Oh Man, know yourself!" a natural law: every step in our inner development must extend our interest in the world in equal proportion, or else we will not make balanced progress. We learn that knowing the world, when we carry it out with a thinking that is alive, strengthens us in knowing ourselves, in "it thinks in me".

We do not become a philosopher in a dusty library full of books, blinking against the sunlight. On the contrary, we become ever more cosmopolitan; the deeper we penetrate into the world of the Self, the more powerful becomes the call for inter-est, for *being in the world.*

Finding the human spirit leads us to finding the spirit in the world-All. The developing human being does not find abstract wisdom; he transforms his human quality of being.

236

Becoming a point in the inner life, in concentrated will-power in thinking, enables us to extend ourselves to a spiritual world that weaves its way towards us from the periphery. Giving ourselves to the world at the horizon, as far as the cosmos, being absorbed in other human beings, in the other, brings us the perception of the point-formed I. The periphery which extends into infinity always becomes point, and diving down under the point extends us into the infinite periphery.

Life becomes cosmic breathing; the inspired cosmic life breath is taken deep within, in a pure spiritual circulation, in spiritualized blood that is received as a stream of thought in the pure heart of *experience,* where, as inner will it can culminate and return again.

"In the rhythms of the world the soul is blessed." [37]

The love for Sophia *realized* by the human being brings Sophia to the human being. She enters into the human heart:

Philosophia becomes anthroposophia.

Uplifted is the stone –
And all mankind is risen –
We all remain thine own.
And vanished is our prison.
All troubles flee away
Thy golden bowl before,
For Earth and Life give way
At the last and final supper.

REFERENCES

1.   1.13 and 2.013

2.   Jürgen Habermas: Post-Metaphysical Thought: philosophical essays.

4.   Rudolf Steiner: Mysticism at the Dawn of the Modern Spiritual Life.

5.   J.W. von Goethe: An Attempt to discover the elements of the theory of colours. Natural scientific writings 1-8.

6.   The Categories of Aristotle.

7.   Written below a portrait of Hegel by W. Hensel.

8.   G.W.F. Hegel, Wissenschaft der Logik (The Science of Logic Part 1), Die Philosopische Bibliothek, Vol. 56 pp. 34 ff. and 53 ff.

9.   Martin Heidegger: Sein und Zeit (Being and Time), Max Niemeyer Verlag, Tübingen, p.3

10. ibid. p.4

11. ibid. p.7

12. ibid. p.12

13. ibid. pp.13-14

14. G.W.F. Hegel, p. 53

15. Rudolf Steiner: Die Philosophie der Freiheit (The Philosophy of Freedom) p. 42f, p.45f, p.47f.

16. Rudolf Steiner, Philosophie und Anthroposophie (Philosophy and Anthroposophy), GA 35.

17. P.E. Voorhoeve e.a. Physiologie van het centrale zenuwstelsel en de zintuigen. Agon - Elsevier Amsterdam - Brussel, p.160.

18. Quotes here from "Goethe's Natural Scientific Writings" ed. R. Steiner, Vol. 3.

19. Rudolf Steiner, Die Rätsel der Philosophie (The Riddles of Philosophy, Vol. 2), GA 18.

20. G.W.F. Hegel, Wissenschaft der Logik (The Science of Logic, Part 2), p.240.

21. Martin Buber, Das dialogische Prinzip (The Dialogical Principle).

22. ibid. p. 143.

23. ibid. p. 183.

24. Novalis, Werke in einem Band, Carl Hanser Verlag, 1984 (Materials for Heinrich von Ofterdingen), p. 395

25. Plato. Selected works in Five Volumes. Symposion.

26. Aristotle, Hauptwerke, Kröner Verlag (Main Works) p.49.

27. Goethe, Dichtungen, Insel Verlag 1982. (Goethe's poetry in chronological order).

28. Thomas von Aquin, Super Evangelium S. Joanni Lectura (I,I-II) (translated into German by W.U. Klünker) p.20.

29. G.W.F. Hegel, Phänomenologie des Geistes (Phenomenology of the Spirit), Felix Meiner Verlag 1988 p.5.

30. Rudolf Steiner, Friedrich Nietzsche, ein Kämpfer gegen seine Zeit (Friedrich Nietzsche, a Fighter against his Time) p.66. Quote from "Beyond Good and Evil", ch. 4.

31. See Selbsterkenntnis ('Self-knowledge') in 'Philosophisches Wörterbuch von Prof. G. Schischkoff, Kröner Verlag.

32. From Dieter, Kühn, Wolfram von Eschenbach's "Parzival", Insel Verlag, p.600.

33. Angelus Silesius, Cherubinischer Wandersmann (Cherubinic Wanderer) EOS Verlag, p.77.

34. Rudolf Steiner, Vom Menschenrätsel (The Riddle of Man) GA 20, p.65.

35. Angelus Silesius, Cherubinischer Wandersmann, Die geistliche Maria (Cherubinic Wanderer. The Spiritual Maria) p.21.

36. Novalis, Werke in einem Band, Carl Hanser Verlag (Works in one volume) p.171.

37. See: ‚The Foundation Stone' by Rudolf Steiner. GA 260, p.282.

LITERATURE

Aristoteles: Kategorien, Lehre vom Satz. Philosophische Bibliothek, Felix Meiner Verlag, Hamburg 1958.

Aristoteles: Hauptwerke. Alfred Kröner Verlag. Stuttgart 1977.

Thomas von Aquino: Super Evangelium S.Joanni Lectura. In der deutschen Sprache übersetzt von Wolf-Ulrich Klünker. Verlag Freies Geistesleben, Stuttgart 1986.

J.W. von Goethe: Goethes Naturwissenschaftliche Schriften, herausgegeben von Rudolf Steiner. Union Deutsche Verlaggesellschaft. Stuttgart-Berlin-Leipzig 1890. Band I, II, III, IVa und IVb.

Jürgen Habermas: Theorie des kommunikativen Handelns. Suhrkamp Verlag, Frankfurt am Main 1981.

Georg Wilhelm Friedrich Hegel: Wissenschaft der Logik 1. und 2. Teil. Philosophische Bibliothek, Verlag von Felix Meiner, Leipzig 1923.

Martin Heidegger: Sein und Zeit. Max Niemeyer Verlag. Tübingen 1986.

J. Krishnamurti: Vrijheid en Meditatie. (Talks Saanen 1974) Mirananda Uitgevers, Wassenaar.

Friedrich Nietzsche: Die Geburt der Tragödie. Wilhelm Goldman Verlag, München.

Friedrich Nietzsche: Also sprach Zarathustra. Wilhelm Goldman Verlag, München.

Novalis: Werke in einem Band. Carl Hanser Verlag, München 1981.

Platon: Platons ausgewählte Werke in fünf Bänden. Georg Müller Verlag, München 1918.

Rudolf Steiner: Grundlinien einer Erkenntnistheorie der Goetheschen

Weltanschauung. GA 2, Rudolf Steiner Verlag Dornach.

Rudolf Steiner: Wahrheit und Wissenschaft. GA 3. Rudolf Steiner Verlag, Dornach.

Rudolf Steiner: Die Philosophie der Freiheit. GA 4, Rudolf Steiner Verlag, Dornach.